THE SHIPS THAT CAME
TO MANCHESTER

THE SHIPS THAT CAME TO MANCHESTER

From the Mersey and Weaver Sailing Flat
to the Mighty Container Ship

NICK ROBINS

AMBERLEY

First published 2015

Amberley Publishing
The Hill, Stroud
Gloucestershire, GL5 4EP

www.amberley-books.com

British Library Cataloguing in Publication Data.
A catalogue record for this book is available from the British Library.

ISBN 978 1 4456 5194 1 (print)
ISBN 978 1 4456 5195 8 (ebook)

Typesetting and Origination by Amberley Publishing.
Printed in Great Britain.

Contents

Preface

This is the story of the ships that came to Manchester. It is an exciting story, with a mixture of success and failure, gains and losses.

The merchants of Manchester were concerned about the high tariffs charged at Liverpool docks and the excessive rates for trans-shipment of goods to Manchester. They decided that the best thing for their trade was to bring seagoing ships up to Manchester. And this they did – via numerous enabling bills and by grand-scale Victorian engineering. The Port of Manchester and its ship canal opened for business on 1 January 1894, with existing clients such as James Knott's Prince Line running to the Mediterranean and Fisher Renwick to London. But it could not readily entice the Liverpool shipowners to use Manchester, and it faced a long struggle to break the Conference lines' indifference to the new port. The First World War finally allayed any lingering worries over the inadequacies of Manchester, and the Liverpool companies then arrived in abundance. Manchester had its own shipping companies, including Manchester Liners, H. Watson & Company and its Palatine Steamship Company, Sivewright Bacon and its Imperial Steamship Company, Manchester Steamship Company, Manchester Spanish Line and others. Business peaked at Manchester in the 1950s but rapidly declined in the 1970s as ships became too big to transit the canal and the port was troubled by dock labour problems.

The author is grateful to Linda Gowans, who checked the manuscript in detail for poor use of English and helped make the story tight and meaningful. Georgina Coleby at Amberley recommended that the text be shortened to tighten the story even further. Acknowledgement of ownership of images is provided where known; I apologise if any have inadvertently been omitted. Where no acknowledgement is given the image comes from the author's collection.

Dr Nick Robins
Crowmarsh
May 2015

Chapter 1

The Political Vision

The [Liverpool] Dock Authority has been by turns in conflict with the Liverpool Corporation, the merchants of Liverpool, Birkenhead, Manchester and other Lancashire towns. Certain it is that the heavy shipping charges and dues exacted by the Dock Board at Liverpool mainly caused the advent of the Ship Canal.

Sir Bosdin Leech, *History of the Manchester Ship Canal Company* (1907)

Manchester was, and is, a proud city with a long and celebrated history. Manchester thrived on the Industrial Revolution, its very name becoming synonymous with the cotton spinning and textile manufacturing industries. The cotton initially came from the southern states of the US until the American Civil War cut off this source. Indian growers stepped in to satisfy demand and shipped cotton by sea to Suez, and overland to Alexandria for onward shipment to Liverpool. Egyptian-grown cotton soon became a cheaper substitute, and this too was shipped to Liverpool for overland transport across Lancashire to the cotton mills. How it irked the Victorian merchants of Manchester to pay landing dues in Liverpool and then fees to Liverpool agents for delivery of the imported cotton. Imports and exports also required shipment by rail, charged at premium monopoly prices, to and from Liverpool.

The idea of seagoing ships navigating the Mersey and then the Irwell up to Manchester was not new, as Bosdin Leech described:

In 1824 Mr. Matthew Hedley, a grocer of Manchester, came to the front as an advocate for a Ship Canal, and in 1825 a company was actually organised. The proposed canal began below Padgate on the Dee, with docks at Dawpool; and passing along the Cheshire side of the Mersey, crossed the Wirral Canal, the Weaver above Frodsham, and the Grand Canal near Preston Brook, thence through Lymm and Altrincham to Didsbury, where it crossed the Mersey, and so on to the south side of Manchester.

The proposal failed to get Parliamentary assent although the second attempt coincided with the bill proposing the Liverpool to Manchester Railway! Verse in the *Liverpool Mercury*, 18 February 1825, included 'Humble petition of the Liverpool Corporation to the Manchester projectors of the Grand Ship Canal':

Oh, ye Lords of the loom,
Pray avert our sad doom,
We humbly beseech on our knees;
We do not complain
That you drink your champagne,
But leave us our port, if you please.

Manchester did receive goods aboard the Mersey and Weaver sailing flats from Liverpool via the rivers Mersey and Irwell and the burgeoning network of canals. From 1824 onwards it received timber aboard barges towed by a steam tug, the *Eagle*, which discharged from the Rochdale Canal beneath Oxford Road, where the Palace Hotel used to stand. The journey inland took over a day and the charge was *2s 6d* per 100 feet of timber.

An article in the *Manchester Gallery of Science and Art* for 1841 shows that Manchester at that date was groaning under many trade disabilities:

Typical nineteenth-century Mersey and Weaver shallow-draught sailing flats (from a sketch by Roger Finch, first published in *Sea Breezes* in September 1949).

At a time when the artisans of Manchester are suffering great privations from the high price of provisions and the scarcity of labour, we find the Corporation of Liverpool applying last session for a loan of a million pounds of the public money to build new warehouses to hold the property of the merchants of Manchester in bond. Where is the public spirit of this great manufacturing metropolis of the world? Does the whole district contain no local patriot to rid it from the wasteful outlay of time and capital in having the goods of its hourly consumption bonded in Liverpool? Why, the very fact of the Corporation of Liverpool wanting a million of money for the purpose of building additional warehouses ought to arouse the people en masse. The money that is worse than thrown away upon Liverpool by Manchester in one year would gladden the hearts of thousands of working families by an additional income of 10s 0d per week. Surely the merchants of Manchester cannot be aware that a vessel called the *Nemesis*, 650 tons burthen, 50 men, 168 feet in length, 29 feet beam, engine 120 horsepower, and drawing only 4½ feet water, has doubled Cape Horn and arrived safely at Ceylon. With 5 feet of water up to our very doors, have we amongst us neither science nor enterprise to imitate the noble example of the people of Glasgow, who by dredging have so improved the navigation of the Clyde, that where they had only 2 feet of water they have now 16 feet, and vessels from China discharge their cargoes at the Glasgow quay?

In 1841, the *Manchester Guardian* announced under the headline 'The Port of Manchester' that the 300-ton brig *Mary* had arrived at the Old Quay Company's Wharf with potatoes from Dublin, returning with a cargo of coal. The Mersey had always been navigable to Warrington and deepening and improvement of channels above there had previously been undertaken by the Mersey & Irwell Navigation Company. However, the waterway fell into neglect after it was bought by the Bridgewater Trustees in 1845 and the Port of Manchester was no more.

The various proprietors of navigation on the Irwell, Mersey and Bridgewater Canal did do one thing right. Each time a bill came before Parliament to enact permission for a proposed railway that was intended to cross one of these waterways, the proprietors insisted on a condition that would enable such a crossing to become a swing bridge should that waterway be made into a ship canal at some time in the future. Furthermore, the proprietors were conscious of existing and important port facilities and shipbuilding interests at Runcorn , the place at which both the Weaver Navigation and the Bridgewater canals entered the Mersey estuary.

By the 1870s, the dream of the Manchester cotton merchants was that one day ocean-going ships would sail directly from Calcutta and pass by the wharves of Liverpool and Birkenhead to dock on the outskirts of the city of Manchester itself. Here, the merchants' perception was that they would have better control over their shipments, the freight rates charged and the local transport of goods to and from the quayside to the mill or warehouse. In short, they would cut out both the middleman at Liverpool and the railway companies. At the time it was also suggested that the railway's monopoly could be undercut by developing metal-plated roadways from Liverpool docks to the principal industrial centres in Lancashire – Tarmacadam

Launch of the three-masted topsail schooner *Despatch* (1886) from Brunditt's shipyard at Runcorn. The *Despatch* was owned by John S. Davies of Runcorn.

was in limited use and not perceived as a reliable road surface until well into the twentieth century. But the long-term vision remained that of bringing ships directly to Manchester.

One part of the equation that the merchants ignored in their vision was the economics of a canal required to bring large ships into Manchester. Firstly, there was the cost of occupying a ship on a minimum eight-hour passage up the canal. Secondly, there were the navigation fees and the rates that needed to be charged for the upkeep of the canal. Thirdly, there was the fee needed to repay the capital loans for construction of such a canal and associated port facilities. Besides, Liverpool had served Manchester's needs well in a partnership between the economic power of Liverpool and the manufacturing skills of Manchester. Why then pursue a course that would inevitably introduce rivalry between the two centres?

The vision of the port city of Manchester would not go away and a determined body of support for the proposed Manchester Ship Canal grew throughout the 1880s. It was led by the cotton merchants, who had two aims: the first was that direct shipment to Manchester would provide cheaper costs than by trans-shipment to rail at Liverpool, and second that efficient and modern port facilities at Manchester would attract shipowners to use the new facilities and so weaken the strength of the Conference lines based at Liverpool and Birkenhead. The merchants viewed the conference system as a means of raising and maintaining elevated freight rates when their main purpose was to maintain fair rates across the conference members and to offer a loyalty bonus to the shippers for use of the conference memberships, so bringing rates even lower.

The Conference system was a means of sustaining agreed freight rates between Conference line members and equitably distributing the trade between lines at an agreed share of the market. Merchants were attracted to the Conference lines, even though their rates might be higher than occasional sailings by non-Conference ships, for two reasons. Firstly, the Conference line ships ran at regular frequency whether it was a period of economic boom or depression. This assured the merchants the transport of goods at regular and advertised intervals. Secondly, the merchants were trapped into a loyalty bonus system rather like the Nectar loyalty card system in wide use by retailers today. This provided the merchants with a percentage return of their overall payment for shipping at the end of the year, commonly up to 5s 0d per ton, so reducing the freight rates to a charge that undercut occasional sailings by low-priced non-Conference ships.

Professor Francis Hyde wrote in his history of the Blue Funnel Line:

> From the point of view of the shipowner the grievance of the Manchester merchant about freight rates seemed to be founded on a misconception of prevailing commercial conditions. It could be argued that in the absence of a Conference system the level of freight rates might have been much higher in times of trade boom and, because of irregularities in the supply of tonnage at such periods, shipping services might have been generally much less efficient. Even under normal trade conditions the rebate paid on Conference line shipments proved to be a powerful inducement to merchants in their choice of ships.

Thus, for example, the rate per ton for the carriage of yarn from Liverpool to Calcutta in 1894 was £1 15s 9d, including a 10 per cent primage fee to cover loading and unloading costs. If the merchant continued throughout the year to use Conference line vessels he would receive back a rebate of 5s 0d per ton, reducing the overall freight rate to £1 10s 9d. It was calculated that any rate for a service direct to Manchester via a new canal would need to be no less than 3s 6d more than this conference rate to enable direct shipments from Manchester to compete with the existing rail services for shipment at Liverpool.

The economics of a ship canal to Manchester were difficult to assess given that usage of the canal would remain unknown until such a facility actually existed. The problem of attracting investors in such a venture seemed fraught with uncertainty. What was certain, or so it was believed, was that the engineering capability was available to build a canal across the Cheshire Plain to Manchester that would be able to accommodate the ocean-going ships of the day. Indeed, it was widely acknowledged that ship dimensions would increase in the future as they had in the past, and that the canal dimensions would need to be generous to ensure a long-term future.

In 1876 George Hicks, a member of the Manchester Chamber of Commerce, wrote a letter to the *Manchester Guardian*. He observed that Manchester and the other nearby towns were suffering under the high rates imposed on goods moving through Liverpool; the Mersey and Irwell rivers were lying neglected as a waterway since navigation on the rivers had been purchased by the Bridgewater Navigation Company.

Hamilton Fulton, a London engineer, reacted to Hicks's letter by submitting a scheme for a 'grand ship canal'. The Manchester Chamber of Commerce considered this plan and in 1877 declared that 'it would be of the greatest service to the interests of Manchester and the trade of the district to have an improved waterway'.

Bosdin Leech wrote on the matter of Liverpool's high dock dues:

> *The Times* in an article on 18 October, 1882, graphically described the incubus on the trade of Lancashire, in the shape of Liverpool charges which the ship canal sought to remove: 'Five millions and a half of people are at the mercy of a combination holding a pass between them and the rest of the human race, and making use of their coign of vantage as the medieval barons did in the embattled toll gates thrown across the world's highways. City, port, dock and railway vie in extortion, and levy duties to the extent of human forbearance. Many millions of material and manufactures pass annually to and fro between the port and the industrious region at the back of it, and on every ton Liverpool has its profit. It cannot be expected that a large population, placed at the mercy of a single port, should sit quietly under it. The more material conditions of the question are much in favour of a ship canal by one route or other, and the very idea of seeing a hundred acres of ocean-going steamers from one's own windows is so charming, that one cannot be surprised at Manchester being possessed with it.'

Support for a ship canal grew, not least through the publication of the pamphlet *Facts and Figures in Favour of the Proposed Manchester Ship Canal*, written under the pen name Mancuniensis (in reality a senior clerk employed by George Hicks). The pamphlet addressed the question of 'how to solve the cheap transport problem for the great import and export trade of Lancashire and the West Riding' and came out heavily in favour of a canal.

Daniel Adamson, the owner of an engineering business in Dukinfield, was persuaded by George Hicks to become the champion of the ship canal project. Sir Bosdin Leech described Adamson as a 'man of fine presence, full of enthusiasm which he had the faculty of imparting to others'. Adamson, who lived at Hyde, called a meeting at The Towers, in Didsbury, on 27 June 1882, with representatives of the larger Lancashire towns, merchants, manufacturers and mayors. Attendees also included the engineers Hamilton Fulton and Edward Leader Williams, as well as George Hicks, who presented some of the commercial and financial considerations of the scheme. Adamson's presentation was summarised by Bosdin Leech:

> Mr Adamson was in good form, and with a strong Northumbrian burr reverted to the wonderful success attending the improvement of the Tyne, the Tees and the Clyde, and felt sure the Mersey was amenable to similar treatment with even better results. If the Suez Canal, situated in a barbarous country and where for 50 miles there was a solid cutting of the depth of 26 feet, could be carried out, there ought to be no engineering difficulties to stand in the way as far as the Mersey was concerned. His own impression was there ought not to be any interruption in the shape of locks,

Daniel Adamson (1818–90), first
chairman of the Manchester Ship Canal
Company.

overhead bridges nor any lack of water for navigation. He advocated coming into
Manchester at a low level and having an underground railway connecting with all
parts of the city for the distribution of goods. He advised all present to read the
pamphlet by 'Mancuniensis', bristling with valuable facts and information, and he
commended the scheme, believing it would be very advantageous to the constructors
and a mighty blessing to Lancashire and Yorkshire.

A provisional committee, later to become the Manchester Tidal Committee, was then
established. It was agreed that a survey should be carried out to investigate the possible
routes, while Fulton and Leader Williams were both asked to produce engineering
proposals for the canal structure. In the event, Leader Williams' scheme was chosen,
possibly more because of his past experience on the Weaver Navigation than any real
technical benefit over Fulton's proposal. With a firm plan in place, the project was ready
to move forward. The committee set about raising funds to put a bill for the Manchester
Ship Canal through Parliament – the project was a step closer to becoming reality.

The next stage was to start to raise funds for the project so that a bill could be put
before Parliament. Support came from local councils, trading guilds and trade unions
as well as the merchants and manufacturers themselves. When the bill was laid before
Parliament in November 1882 four petitions were lodged against it, the principal ones
coming from the Mersey Docks & Harbour Board and the North Western Railway. Not
only was the bill thrown out, but the idea of a ship canal to Manchester was mocked

The intended layout of Manchester Docks in February 1883, complete with lighthouse. (*Illustrated London News*)

Satirical cartoon from *Punch*, October 1882, entitled 'Manchester-sur-Mer, a sea-ductive prospect'.

in the press, not least by the Liverpool daily newspapers, and even in pantomime in performances of *Cinderella* at the Rotunda Theatre, Liverpool:

Prince to Cinderella:
But certain folks in Manchester now dream
Of a vast Ship Canal, so cotton ships
Right up our Mersey can take regular trips,
And land their bales on quays 'longside the Irwell;
But if the waters of that ditch they stir well,
The awful scent, of which you have no notion,
Will taint the Mersey and stagnate the ocean.

A second bill was laid before Parliament and this too was thrown out. Yet the promoters of the ship canal were not about to give up that easily. Despite the fact that their first and second bills went on to be rejected by Parliament, they did not lose faith in their scheme and sought to improve their proposal in reply to criticism, such improvements leading to the ship canal route that we see today. The third Manchester Ship Canal Bill addressed the criticisms received from the opponents of the first two bills and included several new features as described by Leech:

The plans and books of reference for the 1885 Bill were deposited in the middle of November, 1884. They differed from those of the previous year inasmuch as training walls in the river were dispensed with; the channel commenced at Eastham, and was carried through land skirting the Cheshire shore. The docks designed to be made on the race-course were given up, and docks for coasting ships placed in Manchester on the site of the Pomona Gardens. A list of advantages put forth included the carrying of main sewers alongside the canal, and the widening and deepening of the river to prevent floods.

This bill was deposited on 16 December 1884. It finally gained Royal Assent on 6 August 1885. The way forward was now clear for the construction of the canal. Had not the old proprietors of navigation had the foresight to insert a clause in the Acts enabling new railways stating that river crossings would need to be changed to swing bridges should a ship canal ever be built, the Manchester Ship Canal Bill would never have stood a chance.

Conditions attached to the bill included the raising of £5 million before the work could commence. In addition, the promoters must purchase the Bridgewater Navigation Company, including the Bridgewater Canal and Mersey and Irwell Navigation, for £1.71 million. This would allow the proposed canal access to those reaches of the Mersey and Irwell rivers below Manchester and to attain the commercial interests of the Bridgewater Trustees, who had counter-proposed with a scheme to widen and deepen that waterway to allow access to small seagoing ships.

Throughout all the *Manchester Guardian* had remained hostile to the ship canal, but once the bill was finally passed the newspaper changed its tune. Leech again:

Double-ended paddle tug *Earl of Ellesmere* (1857), built by Ogle & Company of Preston for the Bridgewater Navigation Company to tow barges from Ellesmere Port across the Mersey to Garston and Liverpool.

The original three-arch aqueduct carrying the Bridgewater Canal over the River Irwell was opened in July 1761 and remained in use for 132 years, after which it was replaced by a steel swing aqueduct to make way for the new Ship Canal.

About this time Mr C. P. Scott, of the *Manchester Guardian*, was contesting North-East Manchester, and was severely tackled for the hostility displayed by that paper towards the Ship Canal. He pleaded that criticism had done good, and secured a sounder scheme, and he claimed credit as an originator. He said that at an early stage in canal history one of the persons most interested in the scheme came to him and asked, 'Who shall I get to work this Ship Canal?' He thought for a moment, and then he had a flash of genius such things come to the biggest fools sometimes and he said, 'Go to Daniel Adamson'. Now Mr Daniel Adamson was the father of the Ship Canal, and he claimed in this matter to be the father of Mr Daniel Adamson.

The process of raising the money was not an easy one, but by July 1887 the newly incorporated Manchester Ship Canal Company bought the Bridgewater Navigation Company and a month later had also secured promises of £5 million. Disagreement over fundraising, which excluded individual members of the community, led to the resignation of Daniel Adamson from the company board. He was replaced as chairman by Lord Egerton of Tatton. Nevertheless, on 11 November 1887 Lord Egerton cut the first sod at Eastham at a ceremony to mark the start of construction of what was affectionately known as the Big Ditch Project.

Sir Frederick West, first chairman of the Port of Manchester Committee, encapsulated the politics behind the building of the Manchester Ship Canal when he later wrote:

> Of the many things our city has done to inspire a proper sense of pride in its citizens, nothing stirs the imagination so much as the cutting of the Manchester Ship Canal, which turned, as with a magic wand, Manchester, an inland city, into a great port; changed the currents of trade and attracted a wealth of new industry.

The story of how Manchester eventually became a port was summarised graphically in the opening passage from a booklet for schoolchildren in 1938, prepared jointly by the Manchester Education Committee and the Manchester Chamber of Commerce:

> Manchester became a port for ocean-going vessels on 1 January 1894, when the Ship Canal was opened. Before that date the water connection between Manchester and Liverpool was by the rivers Irwell and Mersey. From the seventeenth century onwards the navigability of these rivers had been gradually improved. The growing trade between Manchester, Ireland and Liverpool, together with Liverpool's growing trade with the West Indies, made the need for an effective water link between Manchester and the ocean more pressing.
>
> In the first place, one scheme after another was put forward to improve the riverway. These led to the building of the Bridgewater Canal, which largely replaced the Mersey and Irwell Navigation. The Bridgewater Canal did not, however, meet the need which had arisen for a direct link between Manchester and the ocean. Consequently plans for a Ship Canal independent of improvements in the riverway were drawn up.

One of many meetings, the 'Great Meeting' in the Free Trade Hall, October 1888, held to discuss the prospects of the Manchester Ship Canal Company.

The vision: The Manchester Liners' *Manchester Hero* (1916) inbound at Eastham after the First World War. (John Clarkson)

It then took two years to raise sufficient money for the undertaking. Work began in earnest in 1887. The lowest section, below Warrington, was cleverly designed to be semi-tidal to relieve pressure on the retaining bunds between the canal and the Mersey estuary. However, unexpected floods and engineering difficulties had to be overcome as the work proceeded. Funds ran short, and financial help was given by Manchester City Council, which thus became part owner of the canal and in consequence a certain number of city councillors sat on the Board of Directors controlling the canal. Finally, the canal was opened in January 1894. The undertaking cost £15 million and 16,000 men were engaged upon it.

Chapter 2

An Engineering Marvel

The courage and foresight of the canal engineers was extraordinary. The Manchester Ship Canal project was like no other, but the engineers were able to draw on some experience acquired elsewhere. However, they drew little comfort from the French, who had started work on the Panama Canal in 1881 but had already given up before the merchants of Manchester championed the Manchester Ship Canal. Local experience was on a different scale altogether with, for example, the Bridgewater Canal originally designed for horse-drawn barges to bring 30-ton parcels of coal from Lord Bridgewater's mines at Worsley into Manchester. The design depth of water in the Bridgewater Canal was a mere 6 feet.

The lower section of the ship canal followed the southern shore of the Mersey estuary before cutting inland through the red sandstone of the Cheshire Plain. Numerous problems of water inflow and water loss took place until a dynamic equilibrium was attained between the canal water and the level in the adjacent sandstone aquifer. But most remarkable of all was the setting of the water depth and chosen dimensions of the five locks on the canal, which were targeted well into the future such that they only really became limiting to traffic in the 1970s. The upper end of the canal was designed to take water from the River Irwell to maintain levels. In flood, the flow over the weirs adjacent to the locks would attract ships approaching from upstream and push ships coming upstream away from the locks. Only careful piloting saved many a ship from blunting her bows.

Remarkable also were the daring engineering features along the canal. The Barton Swing Aqueduct replaced the old brick arch bridge to enable the Bridgewater Canal to pass over the ship canal, allowing the coal barges to pass when closed and the big ships in the canal to pass when open. There are many low-level swing road bridges as well, and these all opened majestically for ships in the canal. The Barton Road Bridge was notorious for jamming on hot summer days. Swung open broadside into the sun, the steel structure expanded and all the efforts of the local fire brigade pumping cold canal water onto the bridge were required to get it to close. The two high-level railway bridges at Warrington are impressive structures, and on completion the railway

The River Weaver discharges across the canal into an open sluiceway to the Mersey estuary before the Weaver Sluices were constructed. The adjacent Weston Mersey Lock provided access for shipping between the Mersey estuary and the River Weaver.

company insisted on parking a line of railway engines across one of them to test its strength – and that of the engineer.

The Pomona Pleasure Park, and its celebrated summer brass band concerts, was overrun by Docks Nos 1 to 4 above Trafford Bridge. These wharves were designed for the coasting trades with regular calls from Samuel Hough's and Fisher Renwick's steamers on the London service, G. & J. Burns and M. Langlands & Sons steamers on the Glasgow and Dundee services, as well as numerous calls by sailing ships. Dock No. 5 was never built – it was designed for the stone trade anticipated from North Wales and Cumbria, which never materialised.

Below Trafford Bridge were Docks Nos 6 to 8 and the turning basin adjacent to the timber-clad Trafford Wharf. The main distraction for dockers and sailors alike was Salford Race Course, situated adjacent to Dock No. 8 and separated from it only by a low wall. The race course was later the site of No. 9 Dock, equipped at first only on the upstream side, leaving large parts of the former race course for dockers to rent allotments and, of course, enjoy the inevitable game of football. Here, many a week's earnings were wagered as a home port crew played an international match against a scratch team from some visiting foreign-flag steamer.

Trafford Park, of course, was originally a park featuring a magnificent house, the home of Sir Humphrey de Trafford, with a crystal clear ornamental pond in the magnificent gardens. The park hosted the Manchester Royal Jubilee Exhibition in

1887, and the magnificent glass houses built for the exhibition were subsequently adopted by the botanical society for its annual flower show. Trafford had stipulated that his green and pleasant estate be separated from the adjacent canal between Barton and Mode Wheel by a 6-foot-high red sandstone wall. The remnants of this are still visible upstream from the platform over the Bridgewater Canal at the Barton Swing Aqueduct.

But the wall was a complete waste of effort as the estate was sold in 1897 to a property developer who rapidly created the world's first industrial estate. The initiative attracted the American Westinghouse Electric Corporation, which was set up in 1899 as the British Westinghouse Electric Corporation (rebranded Metropolitan Vickers in 1919) and within a few years employed over half the workers on the estate. Trafford Park also created great wealth and prosperity for Manchester and the North West region, and with it untold degrees of waste and pollution which tax site redevelopment plans in the area dearly to this day.

By December 1887, the first steam navvy had been set to work near Eastham. Work was divided by the contractor into nine, later eight, separate sections that could each proceed independently from the others. Temporary rail tracks were laid to facilitate the transport of spoil and other materials. Sir Bosdin Leech recounts:

> Mr Walker, the contractor, in his Severn Tunnel and other works, had had great experience and he believed in making his workmen healthy and happy. He had a large heart and strong religious convictions, so one of his first acts was to provide adequately for his men. His huts were well built and sanitary, he put up meeting rooms, hospitals and schools of a good type, and arranged for a staff of missionaries, nurses and medical men all along the line of the route. These must have been a heavy line of expenditure to him …
>
> The cutting [at Eastham] was about half a mile distant, and the scene at night was one not to be forgotten. Aided by a good supply of Well's pneumatic oil lights, hundreds of men seemed as if they were working against time to remove a mountain of soil that stood in their way. Steam navvies of the Ruston and Procter type were driving their sharp teeth into the hillside and removing tons of soil into long strings of wagons, which as soon as possible were drawn away to a tip by small engines. At another place Priestman's grabs were engaged in a similar way, and there were numbers of men filling waggons by hand.

Along the line of the canal, land procurement was at an advanced state under the guidance of Mr Dunlop, the land agent. Where the owners refused to sell at the price offered, the two parties were referred to impartial arbitration.

Among the many accidents during construction was that of the switch-lad being run over by the steam engine *Ince* near the stores depot at Norton. The lad had his arm broken and was whisked away to hospital accompanied by the distraught engine driver, who turned out to be his father. Modern-day health and safety regulations would not have permitted many of the working practices. For example: horse barrow roads, a plank laid at an angle of 45° up the cutting bank on which a barrow and a

Construction of the crane wharf adjacent to Eastham Locks. It was used to remove topmasts and funnel tops in order to reduce air-draught for ships to pass under the various bridges across the canal.

Eastham Locks, newly completed and with all equipment and debris removed from the canal bottom, ready for flooding.

Steam-powered inclined ramp at Partington used to remove barrows of spoil from the works and return empty ones.

man steadying it from behind could be lifted by horse and rope with the barrow tipped at the top and returned by the same means – twice per minute! Any man who was injured and lost an arm or leg in the course of his work was retained by Mr Walker as watchman; this small army of men was known as 'Walker's Fragments'.

The hardest ground to deal with was the numerous peaty areas below Warrington, where even the slightest rainfall hindered work. However, Thomas Andrew Walker, the contractor, seemed to be a match for all but the worst conditions. Sadly, he was taken ill in November 1889 and died at his home near Chepstow. But nearly half the earth needed to be excavated had already been removed and the contractor, despite losing its leader, was well on track. However, in October 1889 the Ince section was overwhelmed by high tidal waters enhanced by gale force winds. The water overtopped the embankment between the canal and the estuary, destroying the bank-top railway and flooding machinery in the canal bottom. In due course, the ten sluices designed to clear the water of the River Weaver at times of flood into the estuary were completed. However, much of the trenching in this section was in soft clay and was difficult to work. A head-on collision of the engines *Garston* and *Salford* caused much damage but both drivers escaped by leaping 35 feet down into the trench alongside before the inevitable impact occurred.

Running sands at the site of the Irlam Lock excavation required 10,000 tons of concrete to be laid as a foundation for the lock walls.

Four screw hopper dredgers were ordered from Messrs Simons at Renfrew to dredge the dock system being built above Mode Wheel. Early in 1890, Fleming & Fergusson of Paisley began to erect a pontoon dredger on blocks at the dry base of the canal at Warburton so that she could later be floated off and put straight to work. Steel bridge structures were ordered from Arrol & Company in Glasgow, later to be assembled on site.

Sadly, Daniel Adamson died in January 1890 at the age of seventy-one and was buried in Manchester's Southern Cemetery. Almost immediately after his death disaster struck, as Bosdin Leech reported:

> In consequence of prolonged rains both the Irwell and Mersey overflowed their banks and completely flooded the district. Where the canal cut across the course of the old river, the ends of the latter were closed by means of dams, and filled with the new deviations. The greatest damage was done on the Latchford section, near Thelwall and Lymm; at the former place a great embankment of sand, about 30 feet high, had been raised to prevent the river flowing into the adjacent cutting. On the Sunday night, 26 January, the watchman heard a great noise and found the embankment had partly given way, and the result was that the plant in the cutting, including a steam navvy and forty waggons, were under water. The soil underneath the railway had been washed away, and only the iron metals had been left to bridge the gap. The work of months had been destroyed in one night, which meant a serious loss to the contractor and delay in the work.

Again in November, serious damage was caused by two intense rain events. The first flooded much of the Warburton length of the workings as retaining walls between

Latchford High Level Bridge, with the central section being constructed on a temporary platform before being winched into place.

Dredgers *Irk* (1893) and *Medlock* (1893) were constructed by Fleming & Ferguson at Paisley and reassembled on the dry bed of what later became No. 8 Dock.

the cutting and the Mersey gave way. Reports of a wall of water 10 feet high rushing down the cutting were commensurate with the damage to machinery and plant as well as the engineering works themselves. Labourer huts at Lymm were flooded and men had to be rescued by raft and taken to safety on higher ground. Two weeks later the Barton to Mode Wheel section was flooded by the Irwell flooding overbank. As a consequence, 3,000 men were put out of work while the flood waters subsided and the cutting was pumped out. To make matters worse a very cold spell followed, freezing over the Bridgewater Canal, then the only source of income for the Manchester Ship Canal Company.

In January 1891 it was realised that the company would be about £1.7 million short of funds to complete the project. An approach was made to Manchester Corporation, who willingly pledged the money subject to Parliamentary approval. They were keen to save face with the project and to see it come to fruition. As a consequence the city of Manchester became an important shareholder in the Manchester Ship Canal Company and was invited to send five directors to the company board. In the event, the amount advanced by the city rose to £33 million within the year. The ship canal company had taken over the work from the executors of Mr Walker and was having to compensate them accordingly, so it was an expensive time for the construction of the canal. In October 1891, the Manchester Ship Canal Pontoons & Dry Dock Company was established with the purchase of land near Mode Wheel and at Ellesmere Port. The promoters were from the north-east of England and showed faith in the success of the canal project. Animosity continued from Liverpool, where it was doubted that anything bigger than 300 tons would ever venture up the canal.

The canal was opened for use up to the Weaver entrance when the Weston Marsh Lock was completed and the canal flooded up to Ellesmere Port in May. This allowed the temporary entrance to Ellesmere Port to be closed and the cofferdam at Eastham to be dredged away. Dredging between Eastham and the Sloyne off Tranmere had earlier allowed Mr Platt to bring his yacht *Norseman* up to Eastham in June 1891 and pass through the locks to anchor in the canal below the cofferdam. This was the first vessel of any size to enter the canal. The deep rock cutting at Ince remained incomplete and work on blasting and chipping away continued day and night. On the night of 18 July a fully loaded train was diverted by a wayward switch-boy into a siding, where it toppled into the cutting on top of numerous labourers. Dead and dying were retrieved by steam cranes as best as possible.

In November the first foreign ship entered the canal to discharge timber from Canada and load salt at the new wharf at Saltport, situated just upstream of the Weaver entrance. This was the Norwegian steamer *Deodata*, which was accompanied by a tug. The *Deodata* drew 16 feet 6 inches of water when loaded. In 1893, a peak seventeen ships per week worked cargo at Saltport.

Early in 1892 the nearly completed Bridgewater Lock was overwhelmed by the sea and badly damaged. Notwithstanding, progress was good elsewhere, as Leech reports in his book:

During the excavations for the Manchester Docks and approaches, several huge oak trees were met with; they were of considerable size, and so hard that they resisted ordinary tools, and had to be broken up with an axe; evidently there had once been a forest on the site of the docks. Another feature of the year [1892] was the completion of a dredger, built in the dry, near Hollins Green, by Messrs Fergusson & Company. After floating, she had to cut a way for herself out of the cutting in which she had been built. The dredging department had recently been re-organised and placed in the charge of Mr A. O. Schenk, an engineer to whom the late Mr Walker placed great trust.

At the end of September the City Council Consultative Committee inspected the whole length of the canal. At Pomona the four docks were excavated to their full depth, and the river walls were being put in. The three Salford docks were nearly finished. Mode Wheel Locks were completed, but much dredging needed to be done between there and Barton, largely the result of heavy matter from Salford Sewage Works. At Barton both the swing aqueduct and swing road bridge were nearly finished. The Canal from Barton to Irlam was ready for use with the exception of the hydraulic apparatus for the locks. The Irlam Locks were also finished. At Partington Coaling Basin and sidings two thirds of the work was done.

On 3 December 1892 Messrs Fisher, Renwick & Company of Newcastle-upon-Tyne commenced a regular coastal liner service to London from the new Saltport landing stage. Meanwhile, Manchester City Council was looking at plans to develop a

Construction of the Bridgewater Lock, designed to provide access to Runcorn Docks from the Mersey estuary.

The *Springhill* (1895), belonging to Fisher Renwick, on their London service which began operating from Saltport in December 1892, seen lying at the timber dock at Saltport.

livestock lairage near Mode Wheel for import of live cattle, principally from Ireland and Scotland but also from overseas. Salford was keen to join in and offered £1 million for completion of the ship canal project; Oldham followed with a further £250,000. In the event Manchester increased its loan by £5 million and the offers from Salford and Oldham were not taken up.

In March 1893 Fisher, Renwick's steamer *Blencowe* arrived from London with the first cargo of Indian cotton for discharge at Saltport. By then only those parcels of land beneath the railway crossings remained to be dug out. These were waiting for the railway companies to complete transfer to the five new high-level diversions, and only when compensation with regard to transit times had been paid through arbitration did the railway companies release the old lines. A further problem was failure of the Bridgewater Canal bottom on the Barton side approach to the new swing aqueduct. This was rectified by August, when the first barge crossed the bridge with a cargo of vitriol destined for Accrington. The remaining land bunds across the canal were removed in November and it was announced that the canal would be fully open for business on 1 January 1894.

On 7 December 1893, a party of directors of the ship canal company boarded the Mersey ferry *Snowdrop* at Prince's Stage, Liverpool, and sailed for Eastham. In ten minutes the ferry was through the lock and into the canal. At Runcorn the party was joined by a number of guests, including the Lord Mayor of Manchester, the Mayor of

Salford and various politicians and business representatives. The trip was repeated a week later for the benefit of the press, taking the steamer just six hours to come up the canal to Pomona. The following week freight rates were set; for example, cotton landed at Manchester was charged at 6s 0d per ton, whereas at Liverpool and trans-shipped by rail it was 13s 8d – quite an achievement.

Statistics on casualties were released at the end of December. Apparently 130 men had been killed during the construction of the canal, 165 permanently injured and 997 slightly injured – a high price to pay.

The *Liverpool Courier* finally conceded that Manchester and its 'Big Ditch' were not to be so hated after all:

Honourable rivalry has hitherto existed between the two cities. Let it still continue; the spur of competition will stimulate and benefit both. Above all avoid all petty, spiteful trade jealousy. There be some amongst us whose object seems to belittle Manchester's enterprise, and churlishly criticise the efforts of our neighbours to obtain cheap water carriage, beware of such vain babblers. The canal is constructed. The wiseacres prophesised it would not be. The trade will come to it and to us. Liverpool will lose nothing by the rivalry, if we do not lose our heads in our anxiety to overreach our competitors. There all the danger lies.

It was hoped in Manchester that the jibes about Liverpool building cotton mills at Birkenhead to save cartage, and of sailors singing sea shanties in Piccadilly, were finally at an end. The canal was opened on 1 January 1894 by a procession of ships led by Mr Platt's *Norseman*, with crowds welcoming the procession up to the docks at Manchester where several thousand more people had gathered to witness the event. The business of the canal, to provide cheap transport of goods to and from Manchester, was thereafter pursued in earnest.

Anyone who has sailed down the canal from Manchester will have experienced the illogical but overwhelming fear that the water above the five sets of mighty lock gates on the canal will come crashing down into the Mersey to overwhelm the sailor. The apparent fragile nature of the carefully engineered canal system was its least endearing feature and only time and experience would dispel any lasting reservations about the ability of the canal to host large ocean-going ships. It seems the engineers were also nervous about what they had helped create. Ship canal company chief engineer Hubert Congreve, who lived near the canal at Warrington, worried constantly about the shortage of water in the canal during the relatively dry years of the 1890s. Warren Bruce, in his recollections as docks manager (see references), recounts:

Of course, he was in no way responsible for this state of affairs but it preyed upon his mind to such an extent that one summer night, after dinner at home, he told his wife he was going for a stroll in the garden. He took a revolver with him, walked to the Ship Canal, got onto the high level bridge, stood on the railing of the bridge, shot himself through the head and dropped into the Ship Canal eighty feet below. With his passing a gentle soul went to rest.

Spare lock gates under construction at Latchford. The lock gates were made of durable South American greenheart timber.

Sir Bosdin Leech described the Manchester Ship Canal and the Port of Manchester, based on notes by Sir Leader Williams and others:

The total length of the canal is 35½ miles. It runs for 12¾ miles alongside the Mersey estuary to Runcorn, thence inland for 8¼ miles to Latchford, near Warrington. Here is the first lock, and to this point it is tidal. From Latchford to Manchester (14½ miles) the canal follows the course of the Mersey and Irwell. Eastham, where the canal commences, is 6 miles above Liverpool ... There are three entrance locks parallel with each other, viz., 600 x 80 feet wide, 300 x 50 feet and 150 x 30 feet. These maintain the water level in the canal at the height of a tide rising 14 feet 2 inches above the Liverpool datum, which is rather below mean high water level; when the tide rises above that height, the lock gates are opened, and it flows up to Latchford, giving on high water spring tides an additional depth of about 7 feet. On the ebb tide this water is returned to the Mersey through large sluices at Randies Creek, and at the junction of the River Weaver with the canal; the level of the canal is thus reduced to its normal height. The minimum depth of the canal is 26 feet; the lock sills are fixed 2 feet lower to enable the canal someday to be made 28 feet deep ...

From Runcorn to Latchford the canal is nearly straight, the depth of cutting varying from 35 to 70 feet, partly in rock, but generally in alluvial deposit. The canal passes

Latchford Locks and weir nearing completion, with a temporary railway track running through the open weir sluice. A wooden bridge, icicles hanging dangerously, carries the nearby stream across the canal cutting to discharge into the River Mersey.

through the New Red Sandstone Formation, with its overlying beds of gravel, clay, sand and silt. Retaining walls of stone and brick-work had to be built in these places to maintain the sides of the canal from slips and injury by the wash of steamers ... The canal from Latchford to Manchester is in a deep cutting through the valleys of the rivers Mersey and Irwell. Both these rivers abound in bends, and only small portions of the old course could be used; an almost straight line was therefore adopted, and this involved many crossings of the old river channels ...

The total rise to the level of the docks at Manchester, from the ordinary level of the water in the tidal portion of the canal below Latchford Locks, is 60 feet 6 inches; this is obtained by an average rise of about 15 feet at each of the locks at Latchford, Irlam, Barton and Mode Wheel. These are respectively 14½, 7, 5 and 1½ miles from Manchester. At the upper end of the canal the bottom width is 170 feet, to allow vessels to discharge cargo on wharves without interfering with the general traffic of the canal. The interior locks are in duplicate, the largest being 600 feet long by 65 feet wide, the other 350 feet by 45 wide, each with four Stoney's sluices adjacent. Both the locks have intermediate gates, in order to pass small vessels with the least possible waste of water. They are filled or emptied in five minutes by large culverts on each side, with side openings into the lock ...

As many men were employed on the works as could be obtained, but the number never exceeded 17,000, and the greater part of the excavation was done by about eighty steam-navvies and land dredgers. For the conveyance of excavations and materials, 228 miles of temporary railway lines were laid, and 173 locomotives, 6,300 waggons and trucks, and 316 fixed and portable steam engines and cranes were employed, the total cost of the plant being about £1,000,000. The expenditure on the works, including plant and equipment, to 1 January, 1900, was £10,327,666. The purchase in all of the Mersey and Irwell and Bridgewater Canal Navigations, £1,786,651. Land and compensation, £1,223,809. Interest on capital during construction, £1,170,733. These items with Parliamentary and general expenses bring up the total cost of the canal to £15,248,437.

Chapter 3

Manchester-on-Sea:
Sailors and Seagulls in Piccadilly

Commercial traffic to Manchester commenced on 1 January 1894 with a procession of ships coming up the canal, led by the yacht *Norseman*. There were a few incidents: a minor landslip below Latchford Locks; the steamer *Hazelmere* losing the top few feet of her masts under Runcorn bridge; the Spanish steamer *Granada*, loaded with fruit, grounding near Partington and delaying her arrival at Manchester until after the fruit market had closed; and the Mersey ferries that had been chartered by various groups all had difficulty maintaining steerage at the required slow speeds, while one is reported to have bounced from bank to bank at one stage of the journey! The official opening ceremony was performed on 21 May by Her Majesty Queen Victoria aboard the yacht *Enchantress*.

Pleasure steamers plied the canal in its early days, including the Clyde steamer *Ivanhoe* and the Eastham ferry *Fairy Queen*. The Alexander Towing Company of Liverpool even had the venerable passenger tug *Brocklebank* on the canal for sightseeing trips. She was formerly the United Steam Tug Company's *United States*, dating from 1858, and was later scrapped in 1898. However, the novelty soon wore off and the ships were soon withdrawn with only occasional sailings advertised using vessels from the ferry fleets at Liverpool.

Roy Fenton wrote in *Sea Breezes* in August 1986:

The C.W.S. [Co-operative Wholesale Society] with its headquarters in Manchester had given moral and financial support to the construction of the Manchester Ship Canal, and the Society was represented by the *Pioneer* at the opening of the Canal on New Year's Day, 1894. Her freight of cube sugar from Rouen was the first commercial cargo to be completely unloaded at Manchester Docks, and the *Pioneer* was the first ship registered at the new port. Later in 1894 she sailed home to Manchester with a cargo of currants from Patras in Greece – apparently to meet demand for Christmas puddings.

Samuel Platt's yacht *Norseman* (1890) with the ship canal company directors on board leading the procession up the canal past Barton Aqueduct on 1 January 1894. She is followed by the Mersey ferry *Snowdrop* (1885) with the Corporation on board.

The official opening of the canal on 21 May by HM Queen Victoria aboard the yacht *Enchantress* (1866). (*Illustrated London News*)

The Clyde excursion steamer *Ivanhoe* (1880) came to Manchester in late February 1894 to operate sightseeing tours of the canal and returned to the Clyde in May. Here, very lightly loaded, she is going down the canal at the Barton Bridges.

The Eastham ferry, owned by Thompson & Gough, *Fairy Queen* (1865) took sightseers around the docks and down to Liverpool, returning the next day. She was one of a number of small passenger ships working on the canal in its early days.

The new port was a designated customs port with bonding facilities and its own office of customs officials. However, the response from shipowners was muted, with many preferring to stay as they were within existing Conferences, while some prophesied dire problems for larger ships actually navigating the ship canal. It was also a difficult economic time, with the country stagnating in a period of commercial depression. The magazine *Punch* and other satirical journals continued to mock the new port with mention of sea shanties being heard in Piccadilly Gardens with a backdrop of seagulls, and reports of the new city of Manchester-on-Sea.

During the first week of January only twenty-nine ships berthed at Manchester to work cargo that totalled only some 17,000 tons. The largest ship was the General Steam Navigation Company's steamer *Albatross*, of only 1,450 tons gross, inbound from West Africa, destined to start a new route from Manchester for the London-based company. A disappointing start for the new port, but it also had to be remembered that Manchester had no experienced dock workforce, and the ship canal company had hired stevedores from Barrow, Hull and Glasgow to help teach local recruits how to carry out even routine tasks. When word got out that outsiders had taken the new jobs there was a near riot when a mass of unemployed local men descended on the dock office to demand that the jobs of the 'foreigners' be given to them.

The company managers were all young and largely inexperienced. The ship canal company had been unable to entice senior staff away from existing dock authorities to an as yet untested and novel dock system. Inexperience with working the locks, towage and pilotage all added to the difficulties. In addition, shippers were conscious that there were few facilities for overseas trading in Manchester, the banks were not familiar with bills of lading, and the produce markets were organised only on a domestic basis. In addition there were only a couple of shipping agents already established at Manchester. Little wonder, then, that the start of business at Manchester was slow.

Although the established long-haul liner companies were reluctant to come to Manchester the coastal liner companies saw the new port as an opportunity. Coastal steamers were the only real competition to the landward monopoly of the railway companies. Liverpool was a key hub for the steamers, with M. Langlands & Sons operating weekly to Leith via Stornoway, Stromness, Aberdeen and Dundee, fortnightly round-Britain and twice weekly directly to Glasgow, the latter in collaboration with G. & J. Burns, who brought their own stevedores down from Glasgow.

There was also Samuel Hough running down to London via south coast ports, F. H. Powell & Company focussing on Bristol Channel and London services and the Bacon Line to the Bristol Channel ports and to Wexford. There was an important service to Dublin operated by Tedcastle & McCormik &Company, the Dublin & Mersey Steam Ship Company. They had the new and fast steamer *Blackrock* running directly to Manchester from Dublin. The Belfast Steamship Company had the passenger-cargo steamer *Dynamic*, sailing from Manchester on Wednesdays. However, in September the Belfast service was suspended as the ship was needed elsewhere. The history of M. Langlands & Sons reports:

One of F. H. Powell & Company's cargo steamers running to Bristol, and seen arriving there in this view from the period 1900 to 1906, was the *Watchful* (1882).

... Langlands ... started their Glasgow to Manchester cargo service with *Princess Helena* leaving Manchester Pomona Docks (Glasgow Wharf) on Wednesday 3 January returning from Glasgow on Saturday 6 January 1894 and arriving back at Manchester on Monday. Thereafter the Saturday departure southbound and Wednesday departure northbound became a regular feature of canal life, the service maintained by the *Princess Helena* supported as required by the *Princess Sophia*... Burns inaugurated a two-ship twice-weekly service with passenger berths available aboard the steamer *Grampus* working alongside the cargo only *Seal*. The inaugural sailing was advertised as a grand cruise to view the Canal. Langlands also started to run selected services from Leith to Liverpool into Manchester early in 1894. These carried passengers and cargo, the passengers being conveyed at the Liverpool rate. The *Princess Beatrice* was first to come up to Manchester from Leith.

The new Langlands service between Manchester and Leith was such a success that Messrs P. M. Duncan & Son of Dundee, the owners of the Gem Line of steamers, started an opposition service later in the year, also sailing once a week and on the same day as Messrs Langlands & Sons' steamer.

The Manchester services were considered to be outside the existing Conference agreements and several severe rate wars developed, notably between Burns and

Langlands' steamer *Princess Helena* (1867) was originally the Belfast to Londonderry steamer *Galvanic* and was bought by Langlands in 1889 for that company's service to Bristol.

Langlands. G. & J. Burns upgraded its Manchester–Glasgow service within the year with the introduction of the purpose-built steamers *Spaniel* and *Pointer*. Initially they had fidded topmasts that were removed at Eastham, but the topmasts were soon abandoned and they lived with stump masts only. In addition, D. & C. MacIver had the *Owl*, *Bear* and *Mastiff* serving the Glasgow to Liverpool and Manchester route.

A connection with the Baltic ports was provided from the opening of the ship canal by Liverpool shipping agents and shipowners W. H. Stott & Company, later branded as the Stott Line. Stott owned a small fleet of cargo ships, while the *Flashlight*, *Twilight* and *Eeta* were bought by the company in 1894 to expand the Liverpool base to also include Manchester. They joined the *Starlight*, acquired in 1887, and the *Neva*, which was a much older ship dating from 1865. They were all smaller than 1,000 tons gross but suitable for the trade on offer, bringing forest products into Manchester and exporting manufactured goods on a regular cargo liner service.

The Newcastle company Fisher Renwick, which had started a regular service between Saltport and London in December 1892 (Chapter 2), moved up to Pomona Docks in the early days of January 1894. The company was consolidated under the banner Fisher Renwick Manchester–London Steamers and operated an express cargo service twice a week with the steamers *Eastham*, *Cragg*, *Mancunium* and *Springhill* supported as required by Newcastle-based steamers in the Fisher Renwick fleet.

Deep-sea shipping was not so hasty about moving up to Manchester. However, one of the first liner companies to base at Manchester was James Knott's Prince Steam Shipping Company, later renamed the Prince Line. The Prince company was another Newcastle company interested in the new port. The Prince Line services were varied but a core service was from Mediterranean ports to Britain and Europe as well as to North America. James Knott had been a great advocate of the ship canal project and was puzzled that Liverpool's James Moss & Company declined to extend its own

Mediterranean service up to Manchester. Knott recognised the value of an Eastern Mediterranean service loading Egyptian cotton and calling at North African, Italian and French ports as required, direct to Manchester, which would greatly enhance his Mediterranean interests. Knott commenced a regular service to the Mediterranean in 1893 from Saltport prior to the opening of the Manchester Ship Canal. Although the Moss Line had a virtual monopoly of the Egyptian cotton trade they refused to use the canal, in line with several other Liverpool shipowners.

James Knott's Saltport service sailed regularly to Tunis, Malta, Egypt, Palestine, Syria, Greece and Cyprus. He happily accepted an invitation to use the canal and move up to Manchester and was represented at the opening ceremony on 1 January 1884 by the *Belgian Prince*, which had recently arrived from Alexandria with a cargo of raw cotton. The *Belgian Prince* loaded at Manchester in the first week of January 1894, destined for Casablanca, Tunis and Cairo, to begin a long and fruitful association between this company and Manchester.

Knott was quickly able to demonstrate that the indifference of the Moss Line to the Port of Manchester was very much to his own gain. He also attracted free towage and cheap dock labour as an inducement from the Manchester Ship Canal Company to stay at Manchester. Other vessels on the Manchester to Alexandria service at that time included the *Crown Prince*, *Iron Prince*, *Ocean Prince*, *Royal Prince*, *Creole Prince*, *Swedish Prince*, *Carib Prince*, *Syrian Prince* and *Tudor Prince*, nearly all of them adorned with clipper bows, short bowsprit and figurehead. A. J. Henderson wrote in *Sea Breezes* in October 1949:

James Knott's *Ocean Prince* (1885), registered at Newcastle, on the pontoon at Manchester looking up the canal with Trafford Wharf on the right.

In these early days the company issued grain bags to intending shippers to encourage them to ship by the company's vessels. These bags were stamped with the company's name, and local agents were soon mystified by the failure of large numbers of the bags to materialise full of cargo aboard the ships as intended. It was eventually noticed, however, that numerous local inhabitants in poorer areas of Syria and Palestine were disporting themselves in nether garments neatly marked 'Prince Line', thus providing visual proof of the benefits brought to the Middle East by Prince Line services!

On 30 January, the steamer *Gorji* of the Persian Gulf Steamship Company locked out at Eastham on a voyage through the Suez Canal to the Gulf with Manchester goods. However, the success of attracting the Persian trade to Manchester was short-lived as Liverpool halved its freight rates and the Persian Gulf Steamship Company returned to its regular berth at Liverpool. It was not long, however, before the Liverpool rates resumed their former magnitude.

Trade at ports in the north-east of England was not affected by the emergence of Manchester. The hinterland of Manchester coincided with about a third of the area covered by Liverpool and half of the hinterland of Hull. Whereas shipowners and merchants in Liverpool and Hull saw Manchester as a threat, those in the North East saw Manchester as an opportunity. David Burrell, in his history of Furness Withy, explains how interests in the North East, in addition to James Knott, helped develop trade to Manchester:

It was to be mainly North East Coast interests who responded and established many of the shipping related industries of the new port. From West Hartlepool came Sivewright, Bacon & Company who, within a few years, were to transfer all their shipowning interests from the Hartlepools to Manchester. Christopher Furness played a major role in the formation of Manchester Liners. Additionally moving south from Glasgow, Herbert Watson established a line of fruit carriers from Spain and the Mediterranean to Manchester. Ashore, the Furness, Bacon and Stoker families were also concerned with Manchester Dry Docks and Morrell, Mills & Company, both ship repair undertakings. The Sivewright, Furness and Bacon families were related: Christopher Furness's older brother John and Captain Bacon had both married into the Sivewright family.

Christopher Furness also recognised the port for what it was, a modern, well-equipped port with an industrial hinterland, and he started to send occasional ships up the canal. The Neptune Steam Navigation Company of West Hartlepool sent a few ships up to Manchester from Galveston at the end of the cotton season early in 1894, but this was really too little too late. Nevertheless, it repeated the service for the next season, with sailings inbound from Galveston and New Orleans later in the year. Neptune was owned by the Pinkney family of Sunderland and they managed to bypass the Liverpool merchants by selling direct to the spinners at Manchester. However, it was a cumbersome process which was ultimately bound to fail.

An announcement in the autumn proclaimed that the Manchester cotton merchants had secured a two-year contract to bring raw cotton direct to Manchester from Bombay. The Glasgow tramp company Raeburn & Verel, along with Sivewright Bacon & Company, were to supply the ships needed and the rate would be 21*s* 0*d* per ton inbound and 18*s* 6*d* outwards. Christopher Furness stepped in alongside William Bacon, founder of Sivewright Bacon & Company, to form a company to operate the new service, which was registered at Manchester under the name Manchester, Bombay & General Navigation Company. If outward cargoes were unavailable at Manchester, loading would also take place at Liverpool and/or Glasgow. The Conference lines were appalled at the collective actions of the Manchester merchants and affronted by the action of the various companies and individuals involved. The merchants were delighted.

Even worse was the arrival of the chartered steamer *Rosary* to load machinery for Messrs Brooks & Doxey of Openshaw for export to India. They had a full shipload and were able to undercut the Conference rate of £2 5*s* 0*d* per ton to bring the tonnage rate down to about £1 5*s* 0*d*. This action alarmed the Conference lines such that they immediately brought their rate down to £1 7*s* 0*d* for machinery shipments, but not for piece goods. However, they still had to deal with the Manchester, Bombay & General Navigation Company.

The Liverpool India Conference lines comprised Charles Cayzer and his Clan Line of Steamships, the Anchor Line and City Line, all of Glasgow, and Robert Alexander & Company and the Hall Line, of Liverpool. Charles Cayzer had earlier been quite disparaging about the ship canal and during the 1885 enquiry into the ship canal bill he gave evidence as reported by Bosdin Leach:

> … that he thought the delays in bringing a 3,000 to 4,000 ton steamer to Manchester would be such that it would be far better for a shipowner to pay the railway carriage than bring his ship up the canal. Whole return cargoes could not be got from Liverpool, and there was less chance of getting them in Manchester.
>
>   In cross-examination, the witness admitted that after deducting carriage from Manchester, Liverpool and Suez Canal charges and dues, and Bombay rates there only remained 3*s* 4*d* for carrying a ton measurement to Bombay in twenty-five days, or a little over 1*d* per day, and therefore the idea of charging 2*s* 6*d* per ton for the single or double journey up the canal was singularly disproportionate.

As it happened, Cayzer was to eat his words. The Manchester, Bombay & General Navigation Company was to carry finished cotton goods to India and bring raw cotton and other goods back. However, Furness was soon bought off the route by the Conference members for £11,000 and as a consequence, two of those members, Clan Line and Anchor Line, now became established at Manchester. The first sailings on the lucrative Manchester cotton route took place with Anchor Line's *Hispania* on 5 January 1895 and Clan Line's *Clan Fraser* on 15 January, both to Bombay, and the *Clan Drummond* the next day to Calcutta. The new Indian service attracted a premium bulk tariff of 20*s* per ton, 3*s* 6*d* more than the existing service to Liverpool, but a significant saving on the combined Liverpool rate plus forwarding by rail to Manchester.

The City Line was reluctant to come up to Manchester, but it did send the *City of Dublin* for an inaugural sailing from Manchester on 28 March. Only after some cajoling from other Conference members did Robert Alexander allow his ships up the canal, so that the *Kirby Hall* sailed on 7 November, while the brand new *Haddon Hall* called at Manchester at the end of her maiden round voyage to India early in 1896. Thereafter, the City Line and the Hall Line ships stayed at Birkenhead with Manchester goods barged to them at the same toll as the canal company, as if the steamers were actually loading at Manchester. In mid-1894, the Bombay Indenters Association had been urging Robert Alexander to sign a four-year contract for Manchester piece goods. James Taylor wrote in his history of Ellerman Lines:

> [Alexander] declined to commit himself for so long at a time when the freight rates were so miserably low. Regarding direct loading at Manchester, the Karachi agents were informed that the Manchester Ship Canal was totally unfit for navigation by the steamers now in the trade, and that to go to Manchester would require a considerable increase in the existing rates. He was quite uncategorical when he wrote again… that the Canal had been a failure and the managers had done nothing beyond making high sounding speeches.

Also typical of the attitude of many of the established shipowners was that of Alfred Holt of Liverpool, who again demonstrated the significance of the Conference system.

Robert Alexander & Company's *Haddon Hall* (1895) at the high level road bridge below Latchford Locks, having earlier discharged raw cotton at Manchester at the end of her maiden return voyage to India. (H. E. Tonge)

Holt had always considered the Manchester Ship Canal to be a threat to Liverpool's economic authority and he did not change his attitude once the ship canal was operational. He waited a year to see if the new port would affect his business and came to the conclusion that it had not done so. Merchants in Manchester told him they were not concerned at which port their goods were loaded, but rather which port offered the cheapest through rates. Holt concluded that there was nothing to be gained by using Manchester as he foresaw no likelihood of increasing his share of the trade. However, Holt feared that non-Conference lines could open a new service from Manchester to the Far East, undercutting the Conference lines running from Liverpool and Birkenhead. He therefore obtained permission from the other Conference lines to run a few ships up to Manchester to block non-Conference companies. Francis Hyde, in his history of the Blue Funnel Line and the Ocean Steam Ship Company, wrote:

> The first Ocean ship to make to make the passage of the Canal to Manchester was the *Titan* in January 1895. She was followed at regular intervals during the remainder of the year by other ships including the *Palinurus*, *Palamed* and *Hector*. So, for the time being, the Canal authorities and the Manchester merchants were appeased; but it was a hollow victory. This temporary concession to Manchester opinion on Holt's part had not only safeguarded the Conference and had thereby kept freight rates at agreed levels; it had also overcome the threat of competition in the Mersey and strengthened the Ocean Steam Ship Company's grip on the piece-goods trade from Manchester to China ... After about eighteen months, therefore, the experiment of sending Ocean ships regularly to Manchester was discontinued and the merchants reverted to their old practice of loading at Birkenhead.

Another example was that of the General Steam Navigation Company of London. General Steam normally operated between London and European and Mediterranean ports but had longed to break into the lucrative trade from the Mersey to West Africa prohibited to them by the existing Conference lines. Manchester was seen as the door to West Africa and by providing suitable rates it would undercut the Conference lines. Bosdin Leach recounts the sad demise of the new service:

> The *Albatross* and *Cygnet* and other ships of the General Steam Navigation Company were among the first to come up the canal, and they did the journey from Africa much more quickly than the Liverpool line. They were welcomed by the merchants, both because rates had previously been exorbitant and they carried 30 per cent cheaper, and because of the convenience. One large mineral water manufacturer was delighted that he could send lorries loaded with his bottles to the docks and have them safely housed on the ship, instead of sending them by rail to Liverpool, with all its costs and risks. At first the new line got fair outward cargoes, but then the [Conference] ring swooped down. They reduced the rates about one-third, and told the merchants they intended to drive away the interlopers.

Return cargoes had been difficult and in September the company withdrew from Manchester and retrenched to Liverpool. This angered the West African Conference even more, who threatened to oppose the General Steam Navigation Company on their lucrative monopoly between Bordeaux and various UK ports by calling en route to and from Africa. General Steam at this stage was left with no option other than to withdraw from north-west England altogether. The general manager, Mr Nelson, is quoted in the *Manchester Evening News* as laying the blame at the doors of the Manchester merchants, despite his chairman earlier reporting in the same newspaper that the service to and from Manchester was doing well.

The Conference issue and the unwillingness of Conference lines to move to Manchester was a massive problem for the embryo port. The examples of Christopher Furness, Alfred Holt and General Steam at Manchester are just some of many and the problem of the Conferences had to be solved if the port was to succeed in the liner trades.

In March 1894 the first of the Liverpool lines did adopt a pattern of regular unloading at Manchester; this was the Lamport & Holt Line, trading between Liverpool and South American ports and returning via New York. Such was this company's trade that it then operated outside the Conference systems.

Spot trading did commence quite rapidly. Between mid-January and mid-February the first American cotton consignments arrived; on 15 January 1894 in the steamers *Finsbury* and *Glen Isle,* which had both loaded at Galveston, and shortly afterwards in the *Venango* and *Ohio* from New Orleans. All four were the largest ships so far up to Manchester; the *Finsbury,* for example, was 1,900 tons gross and discharged 4,170 bales of raw cotton. Return cargoes, however, were not forthcoming and the ships sailed for Liverpool to pick up what they could.

Outward cargoes were a problem and the ship canal company pursued an aggressive marketing campaign, persuading industrialists to export via Manchester. Domestic outward cargoes were not a problem, the freight rate from Manchester to London, for example, having dropped from £1 5s 0d per ton to 16s 8d.

The final word on the first year of trading is that of Bosdin Leach, who concluded:

In starting a huge pioneer concern like the Ship Canal, where everything had to be learned by experience, with no similar undertaking to copy from, and where the staff were practically new to the business, there must necessarily be a certain amount of confusion and many mistakes. The warehousing accommodation was insufficient, the railway lines on the docks were incomplete, and there was only one junction to connect with the general railway system of the country. The distribution and collection of goods had to be organised, a system of canvassing for trade had to be matured, and through rates had to be arranged in face of the unwillingness of railway companies to co-operate. A few experienced men accustomed to handling cargo had been secured, but the quality of the bulk of the labour available was unsatisfactory. Added to this the railway and Liverpool dock and town interests were bitterly hostile to the canal, and were only too glad of every opportunity to publish and sneer at any mishaps and shortcomings that might occur.

Dredging was initially an expensive item on the ship canal company budget – the steam bucket dredger *Medlock* (1893) is seen at work at Latchford.

At the end of the first year of trading the share capital had decreased by £5 million. Maintenance costs had been high, with dredging being a major and ongoing expense. The future of the new enterprise looked grim. Future prosperity was only held together by the determination of the company directors to rectify the prospects of the Port of Manchester. A new fruit market was opened, plans were in hand to build warehousing for cotton imports and a spot market for cotton was planned. It was also becoming increasingly obvious that Manchester people would have to become involved with shipowning, as they had at Liverpool, Hull and elsewhere.

Chapter 4

The Development of Trade

As the Great Victorian Depression trudged on, the fortunes of the ship canal company did not improve. But the company could not be accused of extravagance, although there were elements of wastage through mismanagement of staff. The dock office was at the Stretford end of Trafford Bridge, and comprised a series of Edwards the contractor's accommodation sheds and the old wooden chapel from Runcorn. There was no heating and the toilets were rudimentary. This situation prevailed for the next thirty-three years, where only the fittest survived. Wastage was exemplified by dock office staff providing a poor precedent by disappearing off to the pub in the afternoon, and office boys wandering off into the Trafford estate for a swim in the pond in the summer months.

The company had not provided sufficient tugs to assist navigation, and so chartered more in from Liverpool. William Dodd's paddle tug *Hercules*, for example, spent the summer weekends running passenger excursions to North Wales and the rest of the week and all winter operating in the ship canal. The company took delivery of the tug/passenger tender *Charles Galloway* in 1895. It was found that screw tugs were difficult to handle as the stern tug for braking and steering of a big ship, whereas paddle tugs were much more effective. The converse was the case with the bow tug, so a mixture of screw and paddle tugs was used.

The dock estate was accessible only by authorised personnel following the initial problems with unemployed men storming the dock office and later preventing work on at least one ship. As a consequence the canal company had its own police force to secure the estate and to maintain law and order on all ship canal property, including the Bridgewater Canal. The force was initially sixteen strong. The police also oversaw the company fire brigade.

The company also owned 200 miles of railway track and numerous engines and waggons. The track connected with the railway companies' main lines except, initially, those of the Cheshire Lines Committee and the Lancashire & Yorkshire Railway. The former contractor's engines were used on the dock railway at first, but these were slowly replaced with purpose-built locos from 1897 onwards. The new swing railway bridge below the Trafford Road Bridge was completed in 1895.

The tug/passenger tender *Charles Galloway* (1895) served the ship canal company for thirty-four years, after which she was sold for demolition.

Thus a variety of specialist trades were required to make the docks work. It was not only the stevedores that had to learn their trade from scratch; the train drivers and tugmen also watched everything their mentors had to offer. The mentors were poached from the Liverpool tug companies, stevedores from Barrow and Hull docks, the train drivers were 'bought' from the railway companies, but there were never enough experienced men to go round in the early days. And operating the hydraulic gear that controlled the locks and the swing bridges was an art in itself and one that could only be acquired as time went on.

In February 1895, Salford Corporation's sewage sludge carrier *Salford* came up the canal for the first time. She had been built by William Simons & Company at Renfrew and was technically an effluent tanker. Her role was to load the sludge at Weaste and take it down the canal to dump it out of bottom doors over the dumping grounds off Anglesey. Her commissioning was a major step forward in the amelioration of pollution, particularly particulate matter, in the canal. There had been many complaints about smell from the canal waters, not least from the citizens of Warrington. The *Salford* maintained her duties until she was replaced by the *Salford City* in 1928.

The ship canal company still had to face its two major threats: the liner Conference rings and the lack of export cargoes. Before it could do so, however, the Liverpool shipowners and merchants were given another opportunity to laugh at Manchester. On the morning of Wednesday 10 April 1895 the coastal steamer *Harold* left her berth at Pomona to head down the canal. She was a steamer of 682 tons gross, built only in 1891 for Colvils Lowden & Company of Glasgow. The report next day in the *Glasgow*

The effluent tanker *Salford* (1895) was charged with taking the sewage sludge from Weaste out to sea to dumping grounds off Anglesey. The photograph was taken on 23 September 1928 alongside T. W. Ward's wharf at Preston while she was awaiting demolition. (Harry Stewart)

Herald is succinct and to the point:

> The steamer *Harold*, of Glasgow, from Manchester, yesterday morning approached Latchford Locks at full speed, and passing into a lock dashed into the huge gates and burst them open. The vessel dropped 16 feet into lower water below. The gates weigh 300 tons. One was sent to the bottom, and the other remained hanging across the lock. The canal officials succeeded in closing the upper gates and securing them with a hawser, or the difference of 16 feet in the height of the water would have caused serious disaster.

The amount of damages paid by the shipowner for this accident was £13,000. Representations were made by Colvils Lowden & Company to the Manchester Ship Canal Company to the effect that they considered their liability excessive, given the difficulties incurred in navigating the canal. The Manchester Ship Canal Company consequently introduced a clause in one of their bills limiting the liability of owners to £8 per ton. This later became the standard rate of liability for all British docks and harbours.

As it happened, the crowing on Merseyside was not to last long, as the spare gates constructed before the canal was opened were mobilised and the lock reopened on 15 April. The *Harold*, however, was out of service for several months before she was again certificated as seaworthy.

Later that same month, April 1895, the Manchester, Bombay & General Navigation Company attempted to start a service to Montreal with two steamers from the Sivewright & Bacon fleet. At that stage the corporation lairage at Mode Wheel was still under construction and the steamers had to discharge the Canadian cattle at Birkenhead. At the end of the summer season the service was suspended as uneconomical, having received poor support from the merchants in Manchester. It required a subsidy of some form to ensure it restarting in the spring when the ice had gone from the St Lawrence. Neither subsidy nor support was forthcoming and the service terminated.

One of the problems that remained was the lack of facilities at Manchester. Although a cold air store was opened in 1895, and the cattle lairage the following year, there were not enough covered warehouses to attract shipment of piece goods and perishables. The ship canal company just could not afford to build them. It got around this deficiency by a neat organisational twist. A new company, the Manchester Ship Canal Warehousing Company, was registered in 1895; its shareholders invested in building warehouses to the canal company design on land leased at a peppercorn rate and then rented the warehouses back to the canal company at a favourable rate, with an option for them to purchase.

It was also realised that if cotton was to be imported in bulk, then facilities to unload bulk grain, commonly used as ballast for the cotton ships, must be put in hand. Consequently, a grain elevator was commissioned to be built at Trafford Wharf on the Stretford side of the canal, opposite the docks. In the meantime, only 40 per cent of the cotton landed at Manchester came in seagoing ships; the remainder was barged up the Bridgewater Canal from Liverpool. That which did come directly was largely due to chartered ships from Galveston and New Orleans, firstly initiated by charters from the Manchester Ship Canal Company and then independently. The Neptune Steam Navigation Company recognised this as unwanted competition and withdrew its service at the end of the 1895/96 cotton season, despite new warehousing then coming on line at Manchester.

Now, with the support of the newly formed Manchester Cotton Association, Lamport & Holt agreed to import Florida Sea Island cotton via New York on their service to Manchester, which had commenced in March 1894.

Proof that the canal was worthy of big ships finally came when the China Mutual Steam Navigation Company sent two large steamers up the canal. The *Kaisow*, 3,921 tons gross and 370 feet long, arrived in March 1895 and the *Moyanne*, 4,646 tons gross and 410 feet long, in September. However, the China sailings, both by China Mutual and rival Alfred Holt, ceased thereafter and reverted to London and Liverpool respectively. The last sailing was made by Holt's steamer *Tantalus* in December 1895. China Mutual was later taken over by Holts in 1902.

A landmark in 1895 was the start of a new service to the Persian Gulf operated by the Bucknall Line and London's Frank C. Strick & Company. Manchester still had no direct services to the remainder of Asia or, for that matter, any port in Africa. In 1899 the West Hartlepool Steam Navigation Company was re-established to incorporate the interests of J. E. Guthe. The new company also started to trade with the Persian Gulf so that in 1902 the interests were merged and a new joint service from Manchester, Cardiff and London was started by the Bucknall Line (23/60th share), Frank C. Strick & Company (also 23/60th share) and the West Hartlepool Steam Navigation Company (14/60th share). The agreement stated that ships on the berth outwards should be between 3,000 and 3,500 tons deadweight and on return 3,500 to 4,800 tons deadweight. This trade ideally suited the West Hartlepool steamers *Whitehall*, *Ashlands*, *Haddonhall* and *Guildhall*, which had deadweight capacities ranging from 3,100 tons to 4,100 tons.

The Larrinaga Line of Liverpool, a family run company originally based at Bilbao in Spain, began a regular service from Galveston to Manchester in mid-1897. The company was keen to optimise its liner service and saw opportunity at Manchester that supplemented its interests at Liverpool. It later extended the service to include Houston. Until the Spanish Civil War the company's ships were registered either at Liverpool or Bilbao, but thereafter all vessels flew the Red Ensign.

Oil in casks had been imported from Philadelphia and New York since the canal opened. In August 1895, Lamport & Holt drew up an agreement with Standard Oil (later known as Esso) for the shipment of lamp oil from New York direct to Manchester. At Manchester it was distributed by the Anglo-American Oil Company, an associate of Standard Oil. A small tank farm grew at Mode Wheel, next to the site of the Corporation lairage, from 1895 and this was later developed to meet the demands of bulk oil tankers. The first tanker arrived on 24 July 1897 with 3,600 tons of oil for Manchester Corporation to experiment with the manufacture of town gas. A new tank farm was developed downstream at Eccles in 1897 as the trade had increased eightfold in the first year of bulk imports. Manchester became the third-largest oil-importing port in Britain by 1898, even overtaking Liverpool in 1899 when it was second only to London. In 1901 the facility at Eccles moved across the canal to Barton, where a new dedicated oil wharf was commissioned against the near-vertical edge of the canal cut into the hard New Red Sandstone.

In December 1895 there was great excitement. The Albion Shipping Company's full-rigged sailing ship *Timaru* arrived from Melbourne after a long voyage of 160 days, and the clipper *Southern Cross* sailed from Melbourne, destined also for Manchester. The *Timaru* was one of eight celebrated fast emigrant clipper ships built in 1874, principally for the New Zealand trade, and would have been a fine sight passing up the canal under tow. The inward cargoes consisted largely of frozen meat, mainly mutton, and butter. The steamer *Gulf of Siam*, owned by the Gulf Line Association of Greenock, was next into Manchester, leaving Australia at Easter 1896.

The biggest fillip to trade was the formation of the local shipowner Manchester Liners. John Bythell, chairman of the Manchester Ship Canal Company, was convinced that Manchester needed its own shipping line to 'show the way'. Dr Farnie, in his treatise on the rise of trade in the Port of Manchester, wrote:

He [Bythell] was fortified in that conclusion by the failure of successive efforts by friendly shipowners to establish a regular and permanent line to North America. The Canada & Newfoundland Steamship Company could not secure enough return

The Albion Shipping Company's full-rigged emigrant clipper *Timaru* (1874) in the Clyde off Ailsa Craig (from a contemporary painting).

cargo from Manchester. Christopher Furness ... failed in 1895 to buy the necessary steamers for a Canadian service and was frustrated in his earliest efforts to establish a separate line from Manchester.

In March 1898, two directors of the ship canal company, Sir Bosdin Leech and Alderman Southern from the Manchester Corporation, visited Canada to explore the potential for a direct cargo liner service between Manchester and Montreal. They brought home a promise of an annual subsidy of £8,000 from the Canadian government, and obtained support from industry and the Canadian Pacific Railway.

Sir Christopher Furness offered to put up £150,000 as seed money for a new Manchester-based shipping company to trade with Canada, provided local merchants would raise a further £200,000. The prospectus for the new shipping company, to be known as Manchester Liners, was published in May 1898 for the shipment of live cattle, grain and general cargo eastwards and manufactured goods westwards.

Manchester Liners – An Extraordinary Story states:

Two second hand ships were bought at a cost of £60,000 from Elder Dempster and two additional ships were taken on charter from the non-profit making, but Furness controlled, British Maritime Trust. The 'Trust was established to charter out vessels to the regular steamship lines and was placed under the management of Furness, Withy & Company in 1896 (its remaining 26 ships were eventually transferred to Furness ownership in 1907). The Elder Dempster ships were the *Queensmore* and *Parkmore* which had originally been built for the Canadian service of the Johnston Line running

Manchester Liners' pioneer steamer *Manchester Trader* (1890), with a distinct list to port, inbound at the Barton Swing Aqueduct and Road Bridge.

out of Avonmouth. They were subsequently renamed *Manchester Enterprise* and *Manchester Trader* respectively, while the chartered ships retained the names *Straits of Menai* and *Cynthiana* ...

When the *Queensmore* first tied up at Manchester she was then the largest ship to have navigated the Canal. She delivered 450 head of cattle to the new lairage, the Manchester Corporation Foreign Animals Wharf, situated just below the uppermost lock at Mode Wheel. The *Parkmore* arrived shortly afterwards under the command of Captain Parry and had the distinction of discharging the first bulk cargo of Canadian grain into the new grain elevator at Trafford Wharf. This facility could discharge 350 tons per hour and offered up to 40,000 tons storage – state of the art indeed.

Montreal was closed for much of the winter when the St Lawrence was ice-bound and St John, New Brunswick, was adopted as the winter port. Halifax, Nova Scotia, also became a regular call for eastbound ships where a deck cargo of timber assured a full cargo during the quieter winter months of trading.

Manchester Liners' chairman, Robert Stoker, was able to obtain options on two 8,000-ton deadweight steamers building at Newcastle, launched in 1899 as the *Manchester Port* and *Manchester Merchant*. He was also able to buy at a cost of £90,000 a further ship building at Middlesbrough, the *Manchester City*, indeed the largest ship then ever launched into the Tees. She had a length overall of 461 feet, the breadth of 52 feet and would easily fit the length and width restriction of the canal locks of 600 feet and width of 65 feet.

She was equipped with a refrigerated compartment and had removable stalls for 700 head of cattle and their drovers, plus a small number of very finely appointed cabins for six fare-paying passengers. The new ship managed a trials speed of 13 knots and sailed for Canada from Newcastle in ballast. Alas, she nearly foundered off Dunnet Head but was eventually safely returned to the Tyne for repairs after dragging anchors and grounding at Cromarty.

The *Manchester City* first came up to Manchester on 16 January 1899. R. B. Stoker, in his brief history of the company, reported:

How there were many shakings of the head, not in Liverpool only, over the audacity of the attempt. How for the first half mile up the 'ditch' the idle spectators were rather worried but Pilot George Cartwright and Captain Forrest passed other vessels and brought her through the locks without scratching the paint. That night she stopped at Irlam to give the pilots, officers and engineers a well-earned rest – the pilots 'looking as if they had not been in bed for a week, after they have finished the day's work, for their eyes are bleared with exhaustion'.

The following morning the *Manchester City* berthed alongside the Mode Wheel lairage to discharge 450 head of cattle and 150 sheep. Her officers and pilots were whisked away to the Town Hall for a full-blown civic reception with the Lord Mayor. The essence of the celebration was that if a modern, large ocean cargo liner such as the *Manchester City* could safely navigate to Manchester, so too could any of the larger modern vessels then in use.

The *Manchester Guardian*, 16 January 1899, reported the arrival of the *Manchester City*:

Her four telescoped masts and telescoped funnel gave her that appearance of squatness which has become the peculiar advertisement of Manchester ... She was distinguished by her great size from all other ships that have used the Canal. Famous at Middlesbrough as the largest ship ever built on the Tees; famous on the Tyne and on the coasts of Wick and Cromartyshire as the steamer that broke her quadrant during a gale in the Pentland Firth and made her way back zig-zag fashion into the North Sea without the help of a rudder, only to lose her anchors and be driven ashore in the Firth of Cromarty; famous at St John in New Brunswick as the greatest ship that ever was there; famous in Liverpool as a ship built to do that which had often been declared by Liverpool shipowners to be impossible for any ship of her size.

But it was not all good news. The *Manchester Enterprise*, the very first ship to fly the Manchester Liners flag, sank due to a leak in the hull adjacent to the athwartships bunker. Her fires were soon extinguished by the rising water and the ship abandoned. At the subsequent inquiry the story was heard of how the ship had foundered in a gale in the North Atlantic on 14 November 1899, outbound to Montreal.

Descriptions of the loss at the subsequent Board of Trade enquiry included comments by crew members that the ship 'just leaked badly' and 'could roll even in the Ship Canal', which did not help the image of Manchester Liners. There were accusations that the boilers leaked and that the bilges were clogged with debris. It was said that her sister, the *Manchester Trader*, could make better headway in rough weather by going astern than forward, and that she twice took ten days just to get from the Mersey to Queenstown in the south of Ireland! Nevertheless, the enquiry found that the loss was no fault of the owners or the manner in which they had equipped the *Manchester Enterprise*. As for the surviving *Manchester Trader*, well she was a handy-sized ship and, as it happened, remained profitable in the fleet for a further thirteen years.

Manchester Liners was here to stay. The 8,000-ton deadweight *Manchester Merchant* and *Manchester Port* joined the fleet in May 1899 and February 1900 respectively. The equally large sisters *Manchester Corporation* and *Manchester Commerce* were delivered in July and November 1899. And finally, the smaller *Manchester Importer* and *Manchester Shipper* arrived in August 1899 and February 1900.

Until the early 1890s James Knott had ordered ships with clipper bows to try and allay the perception that the Prince Line was nothing but a tramp steamship company. This trend was soon finished with and a series of workmanlike steamers came out in the decade, suitable for a variety of the company's burgeoning liner trades. Sailings from Manchester to the Mediterranean were approximately every three weeks and offered limited First Class passenger accommodation. The passenger fare to Gibraltar was £6, to Tunis or Malta £9, to Alexandria £13 and to Beyrouth (Beirut) or Jaffa £16. At the same time the company developed the Jaffa orange trade, carrying citrus fruits from the Holy Land and Palestine both to Manchester and to London. It was also the first Manchester-based liner company to be admitted to a Conference, for after working closely with the Egyptian Shipping Conference throughout 1898 it was finally admitted into the circle in October that year. This was the first acknowledgement by the Liverpool shipowners that Manchester was here to be reckoned with.

The timber importing trade had spread from Saltport up the canal to Trafford Wharf, where timber arrived from Canada and the Baltic. Wood pulp for paper making was also imported such that by 1897, Manchester was the main British centre for pulp imports. The Baltic trade developed quickly, much to the alarm of traditional shippers importing to East Coast ports. Thomas Wilson & Sons of Hull put paid to the threat by starting its own cargo liner services from Manchester to Russia, to Sweden and to Norway. Thereafter, up until the First World War timber and pulp amounted to one quarter of the tonnage of imports into the ship canal and Manchester docks.

Saltport, with its 700-foot-long wharf, was home to several trades, but it was also the focus of the sailing ships which discharged into lighters for onward delivery at Manchester. Sailing ships also used Runcorn but rarely went further up the canal as they were difficult to tow and most had too high an air draught to clear the bridges.

The coastal and Irish trades remained much as before. A new company, the Dublin & Manchester Steamship Company (Stewart & Lowen) was founded in 1897 by D. J. Stewart of Dublin and George Lowen of Manchester. Initially using chartered ships for a service between its namesake ports, it bought the paddle steamer *Duke of Leinster*, dating from 1870, from the Duke Line in July that year and placed her in service between Manchester and Dublin. She provided a twice-weekly service to Dublin and offered substantial cabin accommodation for passengers. The *Duke of Leinster* was the only seagoing paddler to operate from Manchester. She was joined in 1899 by the former Burns steamer *Hare*.

The *Manchester Corporation* (1899) was one of a pair of ships delivered by the Furness, Withy shipyard at Middlesbrough.

The forward deck of the *Manchester Corporation* (1899) with cattle stalls facing inwards, away from the sea. (Ray Carter collection)

The *Manchester Importer* (1899) with lines of cattle stalls built on deck, both fore and aft. (B. & A. Feilden)

The *Carib Prince* (1893) in No. 8 Dock; note the equine figurehead. The *Manchester Importer* (1899) is beyond.

The *Trojan Prince* (1896), also in No. 8 Dock, was one of the last Prince Line ships to be adorned with a figure head at the bow.

Sailing ships at Saltport in the mid-1890s. Cargo, in this case timber, was discharged into lighters for onward transit to Manchester. Note the figurehead.

The Belfast Steamship Company ran in competition with the Belfast & Mersey Steamship Company, the latter formed in 1891 to offer cargo delivery services. Belfast & Mersey had the cargo steamer *Manchester* built specially for the trade and later bought a passenger cargo steamer as well. In the late 1890s the *Manchester* started to call at Manchester although her place was sometimes taken by chartered vessels. The Manchester service traded as the Manchester Steamship Company. In 1890, the Belfast Steamship Company agreed to external arbitration between the two companies to end the longstanding cargo rate war. In the event, the Belfast & Mersey Company and its associate Manchester Steamship Company were taken out of the Manchester and Liverpool trade, leaving the field open only to the Belfast Steamship Company.

By the year 1900, following nine years of trading, Manchester found itself the sixth most important British port, having risen from sixteenth in its first year of operation. In 1900 1.7 million tons of goods were imported, amounting to a value of £16.2 million, whereas 1.1 million tons were exported with a value of £7.4 million. Quite an achievement for a port that had started with virtually nothing just six years before. An important development was the embryo Trafford Park Industrial Estate with the piecemeal sale of lots for industrial development. New industry was canvassed that did not have the prejudices against Manchester port that some of the more traditional industry still held. It was hoped that the new industries would help develop the export trade and increase the overall use of the port.

Manchester still had no regular liner service working within a conference and it still had to deal with the prejudicial jealousies of Liverpool, Hull and London. But it was now a working port of national significance which had begun to symbolise the strength of Manchester and the north-west of England. It had opened to business at a time of economic recession with the cotton mill owners and the textile industry in general particularly badly hit. The docks at Manchester had directly contributed to lowering rates even for goods trans-shipped at Liverpool or Birkenhead and as such had a positive impact on industry, so helping Manchester and its industrial outliers climb back into a position of economic strength.

Chapter 5

Bigger Ships

By 1900 the Port of Manchester had attracted a range of liner companies running regular services, mainly across the Atlantic to the Americas but also serving Europe and the Mediterranean, Africa and beyond. Many tramp steamers also tied up at Manchester with bulk cargoes such as grain imports and part loads of manufactured goods outbound. The Manchester Ship Canal Company had its own Canadian agent, Mr R. Dawson, and he worked to persuade various carriers to use Manchester. The Manchester Wholesale Provision Trade Association reported that business had doubled as a result of the direct links to Canada, the United States and elsewhere.

The ship canal company was pleased with the trade that had developed although it was still not in a position to pay a dividend to its shareholders. In 1900, it sought compulsory powers to buy the Salford Race Course adjacent to No. 8 Dock in order to construct a new and larger dock with warehousing on one side but open quays on the former racecourse side. In evidence to the House of Lords Select Committee granting the powers was the statement that Manchester Liners alone had brought in forty-seven ships during the previous nine months. In the event, His Majesty King Edward VII opened the new No. 9 Dock in 1905.

In May 1902, rumours of a takeover were hotly denied by the directors of the Manchester Ship Canal Company. American financier and founder of the International Mercantile Marine Company John Pierpont Morgan had indeed had talks with the directors, with an offer to recapitalise the ship canal company provided he was allowed a majority share in the reformed company. The Mancunians were not having that and they sent him packing.

Expansion of the Manchester Liners fleet continued apace as David Burrell described in his short work on Manchester Liners:

The *Manchester Exchange* of 1901, a Furness Withy-built spar decker [i.e. with a shelter deck or 'tween decks rather than a single deck ship] of just over 4,000 tons gross and 360 feet long, proved to be the ideal ship, and between then and 1904 eight sisters were delivered, three from Furness Withy and five from Northumberland [Shipbuilding Company]. They were named *Manchester Engineer, Manchester*

Inventor, Manchester Market, Manchester Spinner, Manchester Miller, Manchester Port, Manchester Merchant and *Manchester Mariner.*

The *Manchester Market* and *Manchester Merchant* were both lost at sea in 1903. The *Manchester Guardian* of 16 January 1903 reported:

> ... the *Manchester Merchant*, which was sunk off the Irish coast yesterday apparently in the hope that her complete destruction by fire might be averted, was the largest and finest steamer owned at Manchester. The value of the ship, with her enormous cargo of cotton, grain, turpentine, resin and pitch pine cannot have fallen far short of £250,000, and even if it should be found possible to raise and repair the wreck, an exceptionally heavy loss will fall upon the underwriters ...

The loss of the *Manchester Market* was reported a few months later, also in the *Manchester Guardian*, on 20 May 1903:

> The vessel left Manchester on Friday 24 April with a crew of 40 hands, 6 cattlemen and 2,700 tons of general cargo bound for Philadelphia. She passed the Skerries about 3 am 26 April ... [Next day] the weather was somewhat hazy, with very little wind ... on the port bow, at a very short distance, the Tuskar Rock and lighthouse were looming up through the fog. At once the helm was ordered hard a starboard and the telegraph rung for full speed astern ... At 1227 the ship hit the outlying rocks on the north west side of the Tuskar and remained fast. She bumped and worked heavily. [Captain Hikins] ordered the boats to be swung out ready for launching and sent the Second Officer to the lighthouse to wire for help.

Two of the fleet were requisitioned as transports to support the Boer War until late 1902, and two others did single trips out to the Cape. Philadelphia was served by a joint service with the Leyland Shipping Company of Liverpool (owned by Frank Watts Leyland) from 1902 onwards; initial sailings were by the *Manchester Corporation*, followed by Leyland's *Planet Neptune*. Two new ships were delivered just before the First World War, the first to be delivered since 1904. They were the *Manchester Civilian* and *Manchester Citizen* and were considered to be the optimum size for the Canadian trade then on offer; although not identical, they were of 4,706 and 4,251 tons gross respectively. Thus, in 1914 the fleet comprised fourteen ships with an aggregate deadweight tonnage of 102,156.

Frederick Leyland & Company, the Leyland Line (not to be confused with the Leyland Shipping Company), also ran up to Manchester on inducement, starting in the early 1900s. The company was acquired by J. Pierpont Morgan's International Mercantile Marine Company in 1901, divesting its Mediterranean interests to J. R. Ellerman although ship names retained the Leyland suffix –*ian*. Under American ownership the Leyland Line was no longer prejudiced against Manchester and so its big cargo liners serving Boston and New York from Liverpool also called at Manchester as cargo needs required. The cargo ships were equipped with cattle stalls as well as chambers for frozen beef, although grain was the larger part of the manifest.

The *Manchester Merchant* (1904), with screw tug forward and paddle tug aft, outbound below Partington.

The *Bostonian* (1896) was typical of the cargo liners owned by the Leyland Line and is seen here loading bunkers at Partington ready for her return trip to New York.

A major boost to the reputation of the port occurred in October 1904, as Sir Bosdin Leech reported in the *History of the Manchester Ship Canal*:

> ... the *Suffolk*, belonging to the Federal Steam Navigation Company with a beam of 58 feet came up the Canal in nine hours. Her cargo capacity was 10,000 tons deadweight and her gross tonnage 7,313 and net 4,680. This monster of the deep brought a heavy cargo from Australia and with two propellers came up the Canal without a scratch.

The arrival of the *Suffolk* marked the start of the monthly joint Federal-Houlder-Shire Lines frozen meat imports from Australia. In addition, Manchester Liners and the Leyland Shipping Company collaborated on a frozen meat run from the River Plate to Manchester and Glasgow, starting in 1904, for which the *Manchester City* was later converted into the world's largest refrigerated carrier. Although this service failed, the *Manchester City* remained on the South American meat run, working from Liverpool and Avonmouth, eventually partnering Houlder Brothers when they were taken over by Furness in 1911.

In 1911, Federal and Clan started running a brand new trio of reefers into Manchester which had been specially designed for the canal. The ships were the biggest yet while the confines of the canal locks which were 600 feet long by 65 feet breadth were limiting. Although the Federal Line's *Suffolk* was once the largest ship to traverse the canal, the new refrigerated meat carriers were much bigger. The *Argyllshire*, commissioned in 1911 for Turnbull Martin & Company, which was half-Federal and half-Clan Line owned, was big. She had two sisters, *Wiltshire* and *Shropshire*, and each was measured at nearly 12,000 tons gross and a deadweight capacity of 12,100 tons on a draught of 29 feet 6 inches. They were 544 feet long overall and 61 feet 5 inches broad; just 3 feet 7 inches breadth to spare in the locks. They had six holds which accommodated over 400,000 cubic feet of refrigerated space, cooled by two ammonia machines and insulated by charcoal.

The trend for large refrigerated ships on the Australian run was started in 1899 by the White Star Line with their 550 feet long *Medic* class, which had a massive deadweight of 15,480 tons. J. H. Isherwood described the *Argyllshire* and her two sisters in *Sea Breezes* in May 1954:

> Accommodation was provided for 66 passengers and a large number of emigrants in the shelter deck. The three ships were designed to be able to go to Manchester and for this reason the lower masts were short, with large tops, and the five topmasts were telescopic and could be lowered down into the 'tween deck. The upper part of the funnel was detachable and bolted onto the lower half by a flange, in line with the tops. On entering the Ship Canal this upper half was landed by a shore crane and left to wait for the ship when outward bound. To facilitate the unbolting and bolting up, a narrow platform ran all way round the funnel below the flange.

Biggest ship so far: the Federal Steam Navigation Company's *Suffolk* (1902) set a new standard for the ship canal – she is seen here outbound leaving Eastham Locks.

Designed especially for the confines of the ship canal, the *Argyllshire* (1911) and her two sisters were the largest cargo liners to come up to Manchester for several decades.

In 1917 P&O took the three ships and their owners over and they did not return to Manchester after the war. The *Argyllshire* ended her days as the *Clan Urquhart* on the South African run from Glasgow and Liverpool; the *Wiltshire* was wrecked on the Great Barrier Reef in 1922; while the *Shropshire* was converted into the New Zealand Line passenger cargo liner *Rotorua* with accommodation for 114 First Class passengers. She was lost in the Second World War. The New Zealand Line also sent its big refrigerated cargo ships up to Manchester, with typical New Zealand names such as *Hurunui*, *Waimate* and *Tekoa*.

Something of a coup for Manchester was the banana trade from the West Indies. Elder Dempster & Company and Fyffes Hudson & Company established Elders & Fyffes in May 1901 to import and distribute bananas. The home port was chosen as Avonmouth due to Elder Dempster's close association with that port, but Manchester was also selected as a UK terminal. Initially, crops would ripen during the voyage and be unsaleable on arrival. It was also not easy to sell a product hitherto unheard of by the British public. In 1902, Elders & Fyffes became shipowners when they acquired three ships on the second-hand market from the Chesapeake & Ohio Railroad Company and equipped them with refrigeration units. These were the *Appomattox*, *Chickahominy* and *Greenbrier*. The *Chikahominy* delivered the first cargo of bananas and other produce to Manchester in July 1902. A fourth ship, the *Carlisle City*, was bought from Furness Withy the following year and renamed *Oracabessa*. The four ships were all around 3,400 tons gross. They were operated in conjunction with the United Fruit Company, splitting their arrival port equally between Manchester and Avonmouth. A special berth was made available in No. 8 Dock for the banana boats. At that time the service was monthly to either port, but the commissioning of the first three specially built banana boats in 1904, the *Manistee*, *Matina* and *Miami*, doubled the service to allow fortnightly arrivals at both Manchester and Avonmouth.

Between 1905 and 1906 Elders & Fyffes took delivery of a further six refrigerated ships: *Nicoya*, *Pacuare*, *Zent*, *Barranca*, *Chirripo* and *Reventazena*. These were all around 4,000 tons gross, capable of maintaining a service speed of 13 knots and equipped with top quality accommodation for twelve passengers. The four original ships were sold in 1909/10 and replaced by three new builds, the *Tortuguero* in 1909 and the *Aracataca* and *Manzanares* in 1911. The fleet was maintained to a very high standard, with glistening white hulls only marred by the odd scratch here and there against lock walls in the ship canal. The trade became so important to Manchester that it became the leading banana port by 1906. Trans-shipment by rail to Hull for Thomas Wilson & Sons' ships to send to the Continent commenced in 1909, leading to a direct service to Rotterdam which started in 1913.

Success at Manchester was short-lived as Captain Kenneth Leslie explained in *Sea Breezes* in March 1967:

> The increased passage time owing to the traversing of the Manchester Ship Canal made it desirable to obtain a suitable berth nearer the Mersey. An application was made to the Mersey Docks & Harbour Board. Unfortunately they were not willing to make a berth available at the time and one was secured eventually at Stalbridge

The New Zealand Shipping Company's *Waimate* (1896) outbound from Manchester having unloaded frozen and chilled goods.

The Elders & Fyffe banana boat *Oracabessa* (1894) in No. 6 Dock. She was built as *Carlisle City* for Furness Withy & Company before being sold to the newly formed Elders & Fyffe company in 1902 and registered at Manchester.

The *Tortuguero* (1909), also registered in Manchester, in the charge of the tug *Eastham* (1899).

Dock, Garston. This was a good site, well served by the railway company and with warehouse and offices alongside the berth. It was opened for operation on 1 January 1912, when all the Manchester port staff were transferred and that office closed.

And that, as far as Manchester was concerned, was the end of the white-hulled banana boats. The service to Garston soon doubled again to weekly arrivals and departures. Garston's gain was very much Manchester's loss.

The CWS imported fruit and vegetables in season, processed foods and chilled goods including meat. The little steamer *Pioneer* was joined on the service to Rouen and elsewhere by the new steamer *Fraternity* in 1903. She was of slightly larger dimensions than the *Pioneer*, and measured 676 tons gross. The arrival of the *Fraternity* in service enabled a weekly departure from Manchester, usually on Saturday. In 1906 the *New Pioneer* (722 tons gross) was commissioned, displacing the *Pioneer* to the Sale List.

M. Langlands & Sons commissioned a new steamer, the *Princess Ena*, in 1898 for their Manchester–Glasgow service. Langlands' Manchester to Glasgow service was then run in collaboration with MacIver but using Langlands' ships. The *Princess Ena* was replaced by the elderly *Princess Helena*, built in 1867 as the *Galvanic* for the Belfast Steamship Company, until she was withdrawn in 1901 when the *Princess Ena* returned with a weekly departure from Pomona Docks at 7 p.m. every Wednesday. The passenger and cargo steamer departures for Dundee, Leith and Aberdeen were also weekly and were taken alternately by the passenger-cargo steamer *Princess Beatrice* and the cargo only *Princess Mary*, although other fleet members were often on the berth at Manchester loading for Leith. G. & J. Burns commissioned the new

The Burns steamer *Lurcher* (1906) maintained the Manchester–Glasgow service along with her sister *Setter* (1906).

Manchester–Glasgow steamers *Setter* and *Lurcher* in 1906 as replacements for the *Seal* and *Grampus*. They both had steerage passenger accommodation. Samuel Hough & Company of Liverpool offered a weekly cargo service to London and for many years the regular steamer on this run was the *Truthful*.

Burns maintained a regular twice-weekly cargo service to Belfast and Londonderry. The Belfast Steamship Company no longer ran into Manchester, while British & Irish offered a regular cargo service to Dublin. The Belfast & Manchester Steamship Company maintained four sailings a week to Belfast from Manchester with the new steamer *Fleswick*, built in 1901, operating alongside the *Manchester*.

On 1 May 1902, the Belfast Steamship Company returned to Manchester to fight the Belfast & Manchester Company head-on. The steamer *Mystic* sailed from Pomona Docks on Tuesdays and Fridays and although passenger berths were not advertised passengers were carried. The *Mystic* was replaced by the *Caloric* in 1910, and she in turn was later displaced by the *Logic*, a newer ship dating from 1898.

The Dublin & Manchester Steamship Company service to Dublin became a joint service with the City of Dublin Steam Packet Company in 1911. The Dublin & Manchester company sold its venerable paddle steamer *Duke of Leinster*, employing the *Hare* for the new joint service, and the City company provided the *Wicklow*.

The Stott Line extended its Baltic cargo liner service to include Norway, Sweden and Denmark. Its older and smaller ships were replaced by the *Duna*, completed for the company in 1907, and the larger sisters *Luga* and *Neva*, which were of 1,980 tons gross.

The Cork Steamship Company ran a fleet of modern steamers with regular departures from Manchester to the Low Countries. The company had started to use

The Cork Steamship Company's *Merganser* (1908) working cargo in No. 6 Dock, with Manchester Liners' *Manchester Miller* (1903) opposite.

Manchester in the late 1890s and slowly built up departures for Dunkirk, Amsterdam and Rotterdam to one every two to three weeks. The *Merganser*, commissioned in August 1908, became the regular Manchester steamer for a number of years. All the ships were registered at Cork.

In 1913, Arthur Guinness had committed to building a brewery at Trafford Park to satisfy the demand for the unique stout in northern England. The brewer had started to send stout across to Manchester in 1904 and the trade developed such that it later started to send chartered colliers to Garston and to Manchester with wooden casks of beer ready for bottling and distribution. In 1913 Guinness bought the collier *W M Barkley* from John Kelly & Sons of Belfast, making it independent of the charter market. She was not converted in any way and was not a great success, carrying full casks to Garston and Manchester and returning with the empties. The intervention of the First World War prevented the proposed English brewery from being built and Manchester, along with London, became a bottling centre for the Dublin brewery. The *W M Barkley* was sunk by torpedo off the Kish lightship in the early hours of 12 October 1917; five of her crew of twelve were killed.

Oil became big news for Manchester during the 1900s when it overtook Liverpool by becoming responsible for over 10 per cent of the nation's oil imports. Both American oil and Russian sources from ports in the Black Sea came to Manchester. Lamp oil was pumped ashore from purpose-built bulk tankers to storage tanks operated by the Bagnall Oil Company at Mode Wheel, taken over by Anglo-American in 1902, and the Producers Petroleum Company (later to become Shell-Mex) at Barton. From these tank farms the oil was distributed by canal barge and rail tanker to the Midlands and into Yorkshire.

The first dedicated oil tankers were designed and built on the Clyde for individual one-ship companies that merged in 1900 into the fleet of the Anglo-American Oil Company, registered at London. They were coal-fired steamers with bridge amidships and engines aft, with a raised walkway over the well decks forward and aft. Tankers were also built for the charter market; one of the earliest companies to enter this trade was the Prince Line. After unloading at Barton they had to come up through Mode Wheel Locks to the turning basin ready for the journey down the canal in ballast. The larger tankers were always treated with respect by pilots and tug masters alike, both conscious of the deep draught of the vessels and of their volatile cargo.

Most of the liner services continued as before. The Larrinaga Steamship Company continued to link Manchester with Galveston and Houston with departures every two to three weeks. The fleet was modern with ships of between 4,000 and 5,000 tons gross, all with the characteristic Larrinaga family names; for example, *Miguel de Larrinaga*, *Asuncion de Larrinaga*, *Mercedes de Larrinaga* and *Pilar de Larrinaga*.

The Prince Line continued to build for its Manchester and London services to the Eastern Mediterranean while expanding its routes to an almost global scale. Typical of the new ships were the *Merchant Prince*, *Soldier Prince*, *Egyptian Prince* and *Sailor Prince* delivered in 1901 and 1902, with a gross tonnage of just over 3,000, a length of 331 feet and a beam of 44 feet. Their operational speed was 10 knots.

The *Asuncion de Larrinaga* (1902) on the canal, inbound above Barton on a regular service connecting Manchester with Houston and Galveston.

The Strick Line remained regular callers, with the service to the Persian Gulf and exports now including oil exploration equipment such as drilling rigs. The West Hartlepool Shipping Company pulled out of the joint service in 1909, leaving it to Strick and Bucknall alone.

Lamport & Holt continued to run into Manchester from New York as the last leg of their service from Liverpool to Brazil and back to Manchester via New York. By 1910 the service into Manchester had increased to weekly.

Elements of the Lamport & Holt service were described by Mr Tom Waring in an article by P. M. Heaton in *Sea Breezes* in July 1977:

> After leaving school he [Waring] worked for a while in the Manchester Ship Canal office at Latchford Locks, and he noted that Lamport & Holt had a weekly sailing from New York to Manchester. In March 1913, he went aboard the *Thespis* at Latchford and asked Captain Ferguson for a position as ordinary seaman, but she had already signed on and he was given a letter of introduction to the Marine Superintendent at Liverpool, Captain Bird.
>
> On the following Saturday, March 8, he sailed in the *Raeburn* as ordinary seaman for Brazil, calling at Leizores where 350 emigrants were picked up, and after four months and ten days paid off with the princely sum of £5 9s 0d, all of £1 10s 0d a month.

Sivewright & Bacon consolidated their interests at Manchester with the formation of the Imperial Steamship Company in 1905. This new joint stock company commissioned the *Oswestry* in 1905, the *Daventry* in 1910 and the *Manningtry* in 1911. The ships were largely employed in the cotton trade from America.

Another new company to be registered at Manchester in 1902 was the Watson Steamship Company, which grew to a fleet of seven ships by 1915. It traded to Spain and west Mediterranean ports. Herbert Watson started in the early days of the canal as a ship's agent when he moved from Glasgow to Manchester in 1893. In 1897 he became manager and part owner of the *Thirlmere*, built for the Thirlmere Steamship Company, and the *Alagonia*, built for the Palatine Steamship Company. Then he chartered steamers to support the two part-owned ships from Spain to Manchester during the fruit season. He finally satisfied his dream of becoming a shipowner when he took delivery of the 1,102 gross ton steamer *Delamere* in November 1902, following agreement with the North of England Fruit Brokers, who had been underwriting the charters. The *Delamere* arrived in Manchester for the first time, fully laden with fruit, on 24 December 1902 under Captain King. She left after Christmas with a full cargo of pitch destined for Sète in southern France. Shortly afterwards, Watson was awarded a contract to carry Epsom salts from Valencia to Manchester at a rate of 9s 0d per ton.

Watson was then able to extend his service into the west Mediterranean: Marseilles, Genoa, Massa di Carrara to load marble, Leghorn, Naples and Sicilian ports. The ships all had Cheshire and Shropshire place names ending in –*mere*; the *Delamere* was followed by the *Thirlmere* in 1904, the original *Thirlmere* having been sold in 1899. Chartering in continued; the steamer *Ragnas* was under the Watson flag for the period

The Imperial Steamship Company's *Manningtry* (1911) inbound at Latchford with the stern tug *Barton* (1903).

Herbert Watson & Company's steamer *Thirlmere* (1904) maintained a service between Manchester and west/north Africa, trading as the Palatine Steamship Company, until the line was taken over by William Lever in 1916.

1909 to 1910. But the trade was a difficult one, as described by Tony Cromby in the *Manchester Ship Canal Review 1986*:

> Our captains were skilled and capable of handling wide ranging problems from port to port. Short of acquiring another pair of eyes, they needed a smattering of local dock lingo, be it Spanish or Italian, in order to get things done. They knew that cases had to be nicely floored out with casks cant and bilged, with good layers of dunnage to get that ventilation right through the stow. The tasks were hard: masters and officers had to be very diligent indeed. Good care and attention slowed the ripening process and got the fruit to market in the best possible condition.

By 1910 Watson had two steamers a week discharging at Manchester. The *Oakmere* was commissioned in July 1910, the first to offer passenger accommodation with four berths available. In October 1911, he commissioned the larger steamer *Redesmere*, of 2,123 tons gross, intended to develop a new trade carrying grain from the Black Sea and Danube, with the intention of strengthening the company. The last group of ships built for the Watson Steamship Company were the *Colemere*, a new *Delamere* and *Flaxmere*, all delivered in 1915. All the ships were registered at Manchester. The *Ellesmere* was the only war casualty, when she was sunk by torpedo on 9 July 1915 south-west of the Smalls on a voyage from Valencia to Manchester with fruit. Then, in December 1916, William Lever completed the purchase of the company following a very generous offer to Watson. Lever retitled it the Bromport Steamship Company, a company established to import palm oil from West Africa and which ultimately would become Lever's Palm Line.

Another major group of ships visiting Manchester were the many tramp steamers working on single trip or longer-term contracts. 'Hungry' Hogarth's Barons were often to be seen tied up at Manchester, and the ships of the Hain Line with their West Country names all beginning '*Tre...*' were also regulars. The West Hartlepool owners were best represented and included many well-known names such as Ropner Shipping Company and some less well known, such as, for example, the Trenchmann Steamship Company. Other regular callers were the 'Z' ships of Turner, Brightman & Company of London. Brightman formed a partnership with Turner in 1878, and by 1900 the company owned fifteen tramp ships. Half were fitted with refrigerated cargo space and chartered to Houlder Brothers for the River Plate meat trade. The remainder were mostly used on Mediterranean and Black Sea routes and it was these ships that came up to Manchester during the cotton season. All the ships' names, save one, began with the letter Z, e.g. *Zamora*, *Zillah* or *Zambesi*. Ten of the fleet were lost during the First World War.

In addition, there were the timber carriers from the Baltic, non-Conference steamers in the cotton and grain trades, and steamers importing minerals including potash and sulphur. A host of foreign flags were seen in the canal in an increasingly diverse pageant as time went on.

A major bulk export from the canal was coal. By 1907, six hydraulic coal tips had been completed at the Partington Coaling Basin, three on the south bank and three

Watson's *Redesmere* (1911) with a full deck cargo of timber destined for Trafford Wharf.

The *Nunima* (1903) was owned by the Trenchmann Steamship Company of West Hartlepool and was one of many tramp steamers owned in that port to visit Manchester. She is seen entering Mode Wheel Lock, inbound under the charge of the *Partington* (1899) with a paddle tug astern.

Turner, Brightman & Company's tramp steamer *Zamora* (1905) traded to the eastern Mediterranean on the cotton run and is seen, deeply laden, inbound for Manchester.

on the north bank. They could each tip 300 tons per hour and were used for export of Lancashire and Yorkshire coal as well as routine bunkering for departing steamers. The tips on the south side remained in service until the 1960s.

The lock gates in the canal were still vulnerable. The chairman submitted the following during a meeting of the board:

> I regret to have to report that there was another accident to Lock Gates. The Norwegian steamer *Barbro* yesterday [Sunday 14 January 1906] at about 1 pm when going into the 45 feet lock at Mode Wheel collided with the lower gates, doing considerable damage but happily the gates were not carried away. The gates will, however, have to be removed and taken to the slip at Thelwall for repairs ... The steamer is now held for bail and her liability at the statutory rate of £8 per ton will amount to about £6,000 which it is expected will more than cover the cost of the repairs.

The costs were duly paid by the owners of the ship plus an extra £300 for expenses incurred by the ship canal company.

Six months later, on 27 June, the steamer *Cassia,* owned by Mawson Shipping Company of Newport, created mayhem at Irlam in a similar incident. The 1,088 gross ton steamer was heading upstream and intended to enter the small lock as the larger steamer *Cheronea* was coming down towards Irlam to enter the larger 65-foot lock. At the last moment the *Cassia* veered off course and rammed the lower 65-foot gates, causing a breach. The canal above Irlam was lowered by 3 feet as water cascaded out through the lock until the upper gates closed in the force of water so severely that they too were damaged. Temporary steel gates were installed and the canal reopened on Sunday 1 July.

The first significant wreck to block the canal was that of the United Alkali Company's sailing barge *William and Arthur*. She was heading to the Weston Marsh Lock to enter the Weaver Navigation, and had on board a heavy cargo of pyrites. The vessel then developed a leak and sank rapidly adjacent to the Weaver Bend Island on the night of Friday 29 November 1907. Not at this stage a danger to other shipping, salvage began by trying to recover the cargo using the grab-hopper dredger *Elk*. This was given up in due course and the wreck was slung and successfully raised on 28 December. F. D. Roberts wrote in *Port of Manchester Review 1981*:

> By request the [Ship Canal] Company then supplied the services of the steam tugs *Minnie* and *Gwennie* to assist and at 10 pm the voyage to Eastham began. Apparently all went well until approaching Ellesmere Port when the lifting sling at the stern end of the wreck cut through the flat's timbers, and she dropped into the centre of the fairway ... two dredging barges were brought to the scene, followed by the Company's ten ton cranes *Camel* and *Dromedary* ... at midnight on 6 January the wreck was eventually raised and secured between the two dredging barges. The next morning the tug *Old Quay* towed the wreck to berth in the sluiceway at Eastham ...

First of the new breed of powerful harbour tugs was the *Cornbrook* (1905), seen approaching Barton Aqueduct, heading downstream. She had a single triple-expansion engine that provided 700 horsepower. (Author)

and on Monday 20 January, the tugs *Old Quay* and *Minnie* towed the wreck into the river at Eastham and beached it near the east dolphins.

Although the Manchester Ship Canal Company had acquired a number of small tugs when it bought the Bridgewater Canal, it could not afford to build new, purpose-built ship handling tugs for some time. As a consequence, a number of Liverpool tugs were licensed to operate on the canal until 1905. Between 1903 and 1907 the single-screw tugs *Bridgewater*, *Cornbrook*, *Mode Wheel* and *Old Quay* were commissioned and the paddle tugs *Barton*, *Irlam*, *Eccles*, *Rixton*, *Acton Grange* and *Old Trafford* also entered service.

Each tug used two tow ropes. At the bows, about 15 feet from the tug, the ropes were bound together to form a bridle. At the stern the two ropes were crossed, so that the port rope from the tug was made fast to the starboard side of the ship and the starboard rope to the port side. This allowed the tug to pull astern and/or to either side with immediate effect. Pulling astern and slowing the speed of the ship allowed the big ship's engines to provide more power than was needed in order to maintain enough water to pass over the rudder to enable steerage. It was important to keep the stern of the vessel in the available centre of the waterway. If the stern got too near the bank it tended to cling to that side, and if the bows were still near the centre of the channel the vessel would run for the other bank. Great skill and care was needed by tugmen and pilots alike.

The Royal Navy saw the importance of visiting Manchester to fly the flag; for example, flotilla visits made in May 1901, March 1907 and on three occasions during 1912. These were all greeted by vast crowds of people wanting to see over the ships – with a recruitment desk strategically placed near the gate onto Trafford Road!

Chapter 6

The Great War and its Aftermath

During the First World War, Manchester provided essential and much-needed port facilities. Shipping companies that would not normally send their ships to Manchester found that they were instructed to do so; they also found that the facilities at Manchester were modern and efficient in every way. The First World War was solely responsible for dispelling the lasting beliefs in the inadequacies of Manchester. The shipowners themselves found that their services were in great demand, and the value of their vessels had increased considerably due to the shortage of available tonnage as vessels were lost to enemy action. Compensation for lost ships was generous and more than paid for replacements, albeit only after the hostilities had ended. But none of these aspects of war can begin to balance the tragic loss of life of the thousands of men and women from ordinary walks of life who died for their country.

At the start of hostilities the ship canal company laid men off in the belief that the port would be little used. In the event, the opposite was the case and within a short space of time it was under considerable pressure. It was the vulnerability of the Thames and East Coast ports to enemy action that upgraded the importance of Manchester, which rose to be the nation's third most important port in 1917 and 1918 and again in 1920. Thereafter, ordinary peacetime commercial activity reduced the port's role again so that by 1939 it was only the nation's sixth most important port in terms of value of goods loaded and unloaded.

Shortly after war was declared the Panama Canal opened. Furness Withy had viewed this new canal as an opportunity to initiate a service from Liverpool and Manchester via Panama to the Pacific coast ports of the United States and Canada, terminating at Vancouver. Two ships were ordered from the Northumberland Shipbuilding Company on the Tyne for the new service, but their delivery was delayed until 1915: they were the *Northwestern Miller* and *Southwestern Miller*. The sisters were placed under the management and ownership of the Norfolk & North American Steamship Company, and set to general duties as required by the Ministry of Transport. Neither ship was to visit Manchester until well after the war.

Federal Line's *Somerset* (1903), with topmasts lowered, heading up the Mersey to Eastham in full dazzle camouflage. She was lost to a torpedo attack in 1917 on a voyage from Buenos Aires to Le Havre.

For the duration of the war Strick Line suspended its sailings from Manchester to the Gulf. The Federal Line still brought its big meat carriers to Manchester and most of the regular visitors continued to berth at Manchester.

A new service between Manchester and New York commenced in November 1915 with the sailing of the Hall Line's *Melford Hall*. The service was a joint initiative between the White Star Line, Lamport & Holt and Ellerman Hall. Outward, the three companies had an equal share on the berth, but the return from New York to Manchester limited Ellerman Hall and White Star to just 20 per cent each, Lamport & Holt taking the lion's share with their existing route from Liverpool to South America and back via New York to Liverpool and Manchester. Thus, for the first time the cargo ships of the White Star Line (now a member of the American International Mercantile Marine Company) were to be seen at Manchester, more often than not alongside the lairage unloading cattle from New York.

Also in 1915, the new concrete grain elevator was commissioned at the head of No. 9 Dock. Although this supplemented the existing American-designed wooden elevator at Trafford Wharf, the new one had by far the greater capacity.

Many ships sailed from Eastham never to come back, many taking their crews to their death. Military technology had moved on and the Merchant Navy now had to cope with the floating mine as well as the submarine and its torpedoes. Losses of ships and men were horrendous despite the convoy system being introduced as the war progressed. By way of example, the home team, Manchester Liners, lost ten ships in the First World War, eight of them in 1917 and 1918 when the U-boat campaign was at

The *Manchester Merchant* (1904) in No. 6 Dock, in full dazzle livery and fully armed.

its height. The *Manchester Commerce* was the first casualty and she was also the first British merchant ship to be lost to a mine. She had sailed light from Manchester, bound for the St Lawrence, but on 27 October 1914 she struck a mine off Tory Island in a channel that the Admiralty had previously declared to be safe. She sank in just seven minutes and only one lifeboat got away. The master and thirteen of his crew lost their lives that morning.

The *Manchester Engineer* was the next loss, to a torpedo fired by submarine *U-44*, which had been patrolling the St George's Channel. The sinking occurred on her return journey to Manchester when she was off Waterford on 27 March 1916, losing not only a sound ship but also a full inventory of American stores that were desperately needed to support the war effort.

Compensation for the losses allowed purchase of replacement ships. In March 1916 a slow 9-knot steamer, the *Auchenblae*, was purchased from Glasgow owners and given the name *Manchester Trader*, her former namesake having been sold before the war. Both the *Manchester Commerce*, bought from Liverpool owners State Steamship Company, and the *Manchester Engineer*, which was bought from the Treasury Steamship Company, also of Liverpool, in May, were named after the earlier war losses in an attempt to confuse the enemy. Both vessels were lost to U-boat torpedo attacks in 1917.

Within quick succession, early in 1917 the *Manchester Inventor* and the *Manchester Citizen* were lost while carrying out their normal commercial transatlantic duties. Both ships were sunk inbound to Manchester from St John, the one captured by *U-57* and destroyed by gunfire on 18 January and the other torpedoed by *U-70* on 26 April. On

4 June the *Manchester Trader* was in the Mediterranean, 8 miles off the Italian coast, when she came upon *U-65* on the surface and was sunk by shellfire. The very next day, 5 June, the *Manchester Miller* was torpedoed with the loss of eight lives inbound from Philadelphia.

The *Manchester Division* and her sister *Manchester Brigade*, both ordered in 1914, were finally delivered just before the Armistice.

Despite all the agony and all the horror of war there were some bright spots. One of these was the arrival of American troops at Manchester. Several thousand American infantrymen and their officers were carried by the Ellerman City liners *City of Exeter*, *City of Calcutta* and *City of Marseilles* from New York directly to Manchester. The three ships generally accommodated about 120 officers and up to 1,350 men. Peacetime passenger capacity of the ships was 230, 146 and 187 respectively. The First and Second Class passenger berths became the privilege of the officers, while most of the men slept on hammocks slung in the 'tween decks. The ships also carried a full load of equipment including vehicles, armaments and munitions, as well as all manner of stores necessary to support the units once they arrived in England. The three ships each made several voyage between late autumn 1917 and October 1918. The last trip, by the *City of Calcutta*, was marred by collision with the British steamer *Burutu* off the Lleyn Peninsula, with tragic loss of life, following the *City of Calutta*'s departure from Eastham on 3 October 1918. The *Times*, on Saturday 31 May 1919, noted that neither ship was to blame for the accident, which was caused by the blackout and poor visibility:

> The collision took place in dark, rainy, and stormy weather, when the *City of Calcutta*, a vessel of 7,653 tons gross, was on a voyage from Manchester to Montreal in ballast. She was manned by a crew of 156 hands all told. The *Burutu*, a vessel belonging to the British and African Steam Navigation Company, of 3,863 tons gross, was on a voyage from Sierra Leone to Liverpool, with about 114 passengers, a general cargo, and a crew of 98 hands all told.
>
> The two vessels were in different convoys, and, in accordance with Admiralty orders, were steaming without lights. The *Burutu*, which was struck on the port side by the stem of the *City of Calcutta*, sank in a few minutes, and about 160 persons, including the master and officers and others on watch, lost their lives.

After the war, victory was underlined by the arrival of the captured enemy submarine *U-111*, which was put on show to the public at Pomona Docks. The U-boat became quite an attraction and was viewed with an air of pride by her visitors.

The Manchester Dry Docks Company had been under strain throughout the war to satisfy demand for repairs. However, this all changed in the immediate post-war years when there was not enough repair work to go round, as Roy Fenton described in *Sea Breezes* in July 1983:

> The Ellesmere Port branch works was chosen for the company's major venture into shipbuilding, which began soon after the First World War. The timing is significant:

The *Manchester Division* (1918), along with sister *Manchester Brigade*, was ordered in 1914 but their completion was not seen as a war priority and they were only delivered just before the Armistice. (John Clarkson)

The *City of Calcutta* (1903), belonging to Ellerman City Line, docking at Manchester in 1918 with nearly 1,500 American soldiers aboard destined for US Army camps in Lancashire. Her 146 passenger berths were occupied by officers while the men slept in hammocks slung in the 'tween decks.

repair work would have slackened off with the coming of peace, yet with freight rates still buoyant, asking prices for new ships were grossly inflated. The design decided upon was the simplest form of seagoing ship, a single hatch steam coaster 120 feet long. The first coaster was completed in April 1920 ... as the *Ben Seyr* for the Ramsey Steamship Company of the Isle of Man ... such a 270 ton coaster represented a year's work for 30 to 40 men. From the management's point of view, having a ship being built was an excellent way of keeping tradesmen employed when no repair work was forthcoming – always assuming that the owner was not pressing for delivery.

A total of four coasters were built, all to the same standard design then in use by various shipbuilders. The second ship was the *Mia*, completed for A. M. Ralli & Son of Liverpool in May 1923; the third, the *Doris Thomas*, delivered to Thomas Brothers Shipping Company of Liverpool in April 1924; and finally the *Penstone*, commissioned by Zillah Shipping & Carrying Company, also of Liverpool, in December 1926.

From 1920 onwards the Harrison Line, whose directors had spent a great deal of effort trying to get Manchester-bound ships excluded from the southern American trades, started to load at Manchester for Calcutta. One of the first ships on the service from Manchester was the *Senator*, completed in 1917. The Harrison Line was joined also by Liverpool's Brocklebank Line. Brocklebank had bought the Anchor Line's Calcutta Conference rights in 1912, along with four Anchor Line ships. Two of these ships became regular visitors to Manchester, the *Media* and *Anchoria*. Both ships retained their Anchor Line names but were adorned in full Brocklebank livery. From 1919, Brocklebank was 60 per cent owned by Cunard and 40 per cent owned by Anchor. The Cunard link allowed some ships to return via the Panama Canal, loading at New York for Liverpool and Manchester. The Calcutta ships loaded with general cargo, principally manufactured goods, and returned with cargoes of tea. Anchor Line ships also occasionally called at Manchester after the war and their *Elysia* came up to Manchester to discharge from Bombay on several occasions. The *Elysia* had 100 Cabin Class passenger berths and was a popular ship on the India service.

The Federal Line continued to serve Manchester, and the first import of Australian butter took place in 1923. However, as trade declined towards the end of the decade the service was terminated.

The Strick Line reopened its Persian Gulf service on a monthly basis after the war. Now a member of the P&O Group of companies, Strick considered that the 1909 agreement with Ellerman was no longer valid. Eventually, and following legal counsel, Ellerman was reinserted into the trade on a 25 per cent stake and provided ships for one sailing in four on a fortnightly departure. Calls at Indian ports were allowed on occasion.

The new Furness Withy service to Vancouver and intermediate Pacific coast ports finally started in 1921. The Furness Pacific Line voyaged through the Panama Canal to the western seaboard ports of America and Canada. Manchester and London were the principal UK ports for the service, and Manchester Liners was appointed agent for the service at Manchester. The first Manchester departure was taken by the *Mongolian*

The *Elsie Thomas* (1922), and the *Doris Thomas* (1924) lying beyond, both belonging to Thomas Brothers Shipping Company of Liverpool, at the Co-operative Wholesale Society Wharf between Trafford Road Bridge and the swing railway bridge. The *Doris Thomas* was one of four coasters built by the Manchester Dry Docks Company at their yard in Ellesmere Port.

Anchor Line's *Elysia* (1908) discharged part cargoes from Bombay at Manchester on a number of occasions. (B. & A. Feilden)

Strick Line's *Tabaristan* (1907) was one of the only cargo liners with two funnels to visit Manchester. She was equipped with telescopic topmasts to facilitate visits but was sold to the Admiralty in January 1913.

Prince, Prince Line having been acquired by Furness in 1916. David Burrell, in his history of Furness Withy, wrote:

> Various other Prince Line Ships were employed on the [new Pacific] service and were joined in 1923 by the new *Dominion Miller* with her pioneer Doxford diesel. The earlier *Northwestern Miller* and *Southwestern Miller* followed together with ships such as *London Shipper*, *London Merchant* and *London Importer*. With a decision to introduce a new nomenclature having the Pacific prefix, *Dominion Miller* was renamed *Pacific Commerce* and continued to serve with new ships [all with Pacific names] specially designed for the service.

The London names were reserved for the Furness transatlantic vessels mainly based at London and the Pacific names for the Panama Canal to Vancouver service. The new *Pacific Trader* and *Pacific Shipper* were delivered in 1924 with the same Doxford engine coupled to a single propeller. More new ships were planned to increase the frequency of the service from monthly to fortnightly.

In 1924, a regular service was begun to Cape Town by the Clan Line. Clan had been operating out of Manchester to India via the Suez Canal since the early days of the port and it was a logical extension that they should start to serve South Africa from Manchester as well as from Liverpool and Glasgow. There were also the regular services to India and the Persian Gulf. In March 1925, for example, Clan Line advertised the

The *Pacific Shipper* (1924) having backed out of No. 9 Dock is seen turning ready to enter Mode Wheel Lock.

The *Clan Macdonald* (1897) was the first of the Clan Line's turret ships that were built by William Doxford on the Tyne.

Clan MacWhirter and *Clan Urquhart* sailing for Bombay and the Persian Gulf, loading also at Newport, Glasgow and finally Birkenhead, and the *Clan MacPhee* and *Clan Murray* for Colombo, Madras and Calcutta, loading also at Glasgow and Birkenhead. Both services were then scheduled at fortnightly intervals. The *Clan Urquhart* was a Doxford-built turret ship completed in 1899. Turret ships had a narrow main deck flanked by harbour decks in order to qualify for cheaper transit fees in the Suez Canal, the fees being based on the width of the main deck. However, they also had stability problems so that bulk cargoes could not be carried safely above the level of the harbour deck.

From the mid-1920s onwards a variety of liner companies started to work part-cargoes at Manchester in response to demand from shippers. For the first time the cargo liners of the Pacific Steam Navigation Company and the Royal Mail Line came up the canal, bringing goods from both the Pacific coast of South America and the Atlantic coast ports.

The United States Lines started to use the port in the late 1920s. This new company was formed in 1921 in an attempt to overcome the inability of the United States Mail Steamship Company to fulfil its obligations to the United States Shipping Board. It was originally managed by Moore & McCormack, the Roosevelt Steamship Company and United American Lines, but in 1923 the managing partners resigned and the loss-making company was managed by the United States Shipping Board. The United States Lines continued to make a financial loss and was sold in 1929 to P. W. Chapman & Company, who failed to meet payments. Consequently, in 1931 the United States

The United American Line's *West Cressey* (1918), having unloaded at Manchester, outbound at Barton ready for coaling at Partington and then on to Liverpool and Glasgow to load for the return voyage to New York.

Lines was taken over by a combination of the Roosevelt Steamship Company, R. Stanley Dollar and Kenneth D. Dawson, until International Mercantile Marine gained control of the company in 1934. Nevertheless, a regular liner service was established from New York to Manchester, loading at Liverpool on return.

In 1927 Houlder Brothers restarted its service between Manchester and the River Plate ports, bringing chilled meat into Manchester. Manchester Liners was the local agent.

All the existing liner services continued after the First World War, including Lamport & Holt and, of course, Manchester Liners. Manchester Liners took delivery of the large turbine steamer *Manchester Regiment* in 1922. She was turbine driven and had capacious holds (11,572 tons deadweight) that had to be filled on each voyage if a profit was to be assured. Her contract price was £458,600, a significant part of which was the cost of her engines.

Prince Line served numerous Mediterranean ports with ships such as *Syrian Prince*, *Soldier Prince* and *Cyprian Prince*. In March 1920, the *Algerian Prince* sailed from Manchester on the advertised service 'Manchester to Tunis, Malta and Alexandria direct, also Jaffa, Haifa, Beyrout, Tripoli, Lattakia, Alexandretta, Mirsyne and Cyprus'. War losses on the Mediterranean service, including the *Egyptian Prince* sunk by explosives on a voyage to Manchester from Alexandria in May 1917, were replaced in 1919 by the acquisition of three C-Class Wartime Standard Ships: the *Algerian Prince*, formerly the *War Isthmus*, the *Cyprian Prince* built as the *War Planet* and the *Syrian Prince*, formerly the *War Rock*. In the early 1920s the Mediterranean service was supplemented by the addition of the *Italian Prince*, *Egyptian Prince* and *Lancastriain Prince*, all new ships transferred from the Furness Withy fleet.

R. C. Stallard wrote an account of a voyage by Prince Line in *Sea Breezes* in March 1978:

I was appointed purser of the steamer *Sailor Prince* for the coastal voyage from Manchester to Antwerp and thence to London, where she loaded for the usual Mediterranean ports, so there was quite a lot of loading information to pick up. The ship was even then very old. She was built in 1907 as the *Glendevon* for J. Gardiner & Company and in 1917 the whole fleet was bought by Furness Withy and all the ships received 'Prince' names ... I signed on at Manchester on 20 May 1925 and we sailed at 5.15 pm, only going as far as Partington Coaling Basin ... We got there at 8.15 and coaling started almost immediately, going on non-stop until 12.00 next day ... That morning I went a short walk and came upon a pretty little village which turned out to be Partington ...

We left Partington the second day at 12.30 noon just after coaling had finished and proceeded slowly down the Canal which was quite an experience. I have been up and down the Manchester Ship Canal many times since, but it is not very picturesque, the scene being mainly industrial although at that time there were flashes of countryside. We eventually got to Eastham and left the Canal at 8.45 pm, passing Liverpool at 10.20. My first night at sea was not too bad but my diary indicates that I awoke at 4 am with the cabin lit up by the Skerries lighthouse [off Anglesey] ... The fine weather gave way to gale conditions as we approached Land's End and the ship was very lively being in ballast ... we arrived at Antwerp at 6.30 pm on 24 May.

The Cunard Steamship Company became further involved with the ship canal in May 1916 when they, jointly with Ellerman, bought from the Watson Steamship Company (Palatine Shipping Company) of Manchester its interests in the Manchester to Marseilles and west Italian coast ports service. The new owners appointed Herbert Watson & Company as loading brokers at Manchester and the service commenced in June. Watson had sold its other shipping interests to William Lever in 1915, the ships being converted to palm oil carriers for the West African coast ports' route to the Mersey (Chapter 5).

After the war Herbert Watson started the short-lived Manchester Spanish Line with two Norwegian steamers on time charter. A new steamer, the *Delamere*, 1,662 tons gross, was built for the company at Schiedam and commissioned in November 1925. Tony Cromby, in the *Manchester Ship Canal Review 1986*, reported:

> ... the position out in Spain had completely altered owing to the Revolution and other matters. Societies had sprung up governing the shipping of fruit, so the Spanish Government stepped in and together with these societies did all the chartering themselves. Wherever we sent our three steamers into Spanish ports, we were on many occasions baulked in getting cargo – except at a ruinous rate. Eventually the Manchester Spanish Line sold the *Delamere* after only 18 months' running.

There was an increase in foreign flag vessels coming up to Manchester in the early 1920s. This reflected the increasingly diverse interests of the shippers at Manchester and also the ever-increasing competition from European shipowners.

Coastal and cross-Irish Sea traffic continued to grow. Guinness lost their first steamer, the *W M Barkley*, during the war, but acquired three new colliers from Kelly of Belfast during the hostilities. Of these, the *Carrowdore* received cooling equipment in 1914 and served between Dublin and London and Dublin and Garston or Manchester during the war. The other two, the *Clareisland* and *Clarecastle*, were released from government service only in July 1919, when they too started to come up to Manchester. They were steadier ships in a heavy sea than their older sister as they had 6 inches greater depth and 6 inches less beam. The ships arrived loaded with casks of stout and returned with empty casks and sacked barley to supply the brewery in Dublin.

M. Langlands & Sons was able to resume sailings to Glasgow once the *Princess Louise* and *Princess Ena* had been refurbished. However, the company was soon bought out by Coast Lines. The *Princess Louise* was renamed *Clyde Coast* but remained on the Glasgow to Liverpool and Manchester service; she was again renamed *Setter* in 1923. A quartet of cargo ships then being built for Langlands was eventually delivered with a variety of Coast Lines names for use in the group on cross-Irish Sea duties as well as on the Glasgow to Liverpool and Manchester route. One of them was launched as the *Redbreast* for G. & J. Burns and took up service between Manchester and Glasgow in December 1920. The old *Setter* (Chapter 4) had been lost to a torpedo in September

One of the many foreign flag vessels using the canal in the early 1920s was the *Ragnhild* (1919) of Copenhagen, seen at the Northwich Road Bridge. She was owned by A/S D/S Torm, a company still very active in the shipping industry to this day.

Langlands' *Princess Ena* (1898), seen at Pomona Docks, was the regular steamer on the Manchester to Glasgow run before the First World War.

1918 while on passage from Manchester to Glasgow, while her sister the *Lurcher* was transferred to the British & Irish Steam Packet Company in 1920 and renamed *Lady Meath*. Sisters *Gorilla* and *Lurcher*, from the quartet led by the *Redbreast*, also served on the Manchester to Glasgow twice-weekly shuttle so that at any time two ships were deployed on the route. The service was advertised under the banner Burns-Langlands Service. In 1925 it was rebranded under the Coast Lines name and the *Redbreast* was renamed *Sutherland Coast*, the *Gorilla* became the *Cumberland Coast* and the *Lurcher* the *Scottish Coast*, all three now adorned in the Coast Lines livery of black funnel with a white chevron.

The Belfast Steamship Company ran twice a week from Manchester using a variety of steamers, although the *Hampshire Coast*, deployed in 1920, remained on the route for some years. She was built in 1911 for F. H. Powell & Company, one of the three original companies that became Coast Lines in January 1917 when Powell, Bacon & Hough was taken over by the Royal Mail Group. Samuel Hough, of course, was a regular user of Manchester with its liner service to London. A dedicated Manchester 'Belfast boat' arrived in the form of the *Dynamic* in October 1922; she was yet another one-time Langlands ship, acquired by them from the Aberdeen, Leith & Moray Firth Steam Shipping Company as the *James Crombie* and dating from 1904. She stayed on the Manchester–Belfast service more or less continually throughout the 1920s and into the 1930s, when she was renamed *Ulster Star*.

In October 1919 the joint Dublin & Manchester Company and City of Dublin Company service to Dublin was acquired by the British & Irish Steam Packet Company. With it came the steamer *Wicklow*, which for the moment remained on Manchester duties after being renamed the *Lady Wicklow*. The steamer *Hare* had been lost in the war in December 1917, inbound from Dublin to Manchester. Also, in 1919 Tedcastle & McCormick came under B&I ownership along with the steamer *Blackrock*. Thus the two Dublin competitors now came under one roof.

The various diverse coasting company liner services were consolidated, with Belfast Steam, B&I and Coast Lines providing both the Irish and domestic services, and all companies now owned by Coast Lines as part of the Royal Mail Group. However, the Belfast & Mersey Steamship Company was again able to return to trade after having been banished for fifteen years in 1900 by the Belfast Steamship Company. And this it did, using its own steamer the *Manchester* and occasional chartered ships to trade between Belfast, Liverpool and Manchester. The service from Manchester was weekly. The company focussed on the cattle trade inbound to the Birkenhead lairage and specialised deliveries and collections of general goods at Liverpool and Manchester.

Fisher Renwick & Company Manchester–London Steamers continued to run between Manchester and London, with a call at Southampton on some voyages. In the early 1920s the company focussed on developing a road haulage and distribution network centred on Manchester to provide direct connections to the Midlands and elsewhere. Two new ships, the *Sapper* and *Sentry*, were delivered in 1923 and 1924. Although the service had increased from twice weekly to three times a week in the early 1900s, it was pared back to twice a week with the slowdown in the economy in the early 1920s.

The Stott Line had lost the steamer *Duna* when she was wrecked off South Ronaldsay in July 1912. After the war the larger and more modern steamers *Luga* and *Neva* continued to run to the Baltic and Scandinavia, but only came up to Manchester at irregular intervals as cargo demanded. The downturn in trade forced the *Luga* to be sold in 1922, followed by the *Neva* two years later when W. H. Stott & Company reverted to their agency work at Liverpool, looking after the local interests of the Finland Steamship Company, the Swedish Johnson Line and others. One consequence of this was that the Finland Steamship Company took over Stott's interests at Manchester and started to come up to Manchester as required.

An important new development occurred in 1922 with the formation of the British & Continental Steamship Company as the successor to the Cork Steamship Company. The Cork Steamship Company was owned by Amalgamated Industries, but the post-war collapse of the owner's various interests and the mortgaging of all its ships indicated that the shipping interests would not survive. The company's local agents in Liverpool, Glasgow, Belfast, Antwerp and Rotterdam had vested interests in the company's survival and duly offered to purchase the fleet of fifteen ships, six of which had been built since the war, plus the goodwill of the business, for £350,000. The bid was successful and the company was retitled British & Continental Steamship Company to better reflect its business. Manchester became a more frequent call for the ships on their services to Amsterdam, Rotterdam and Dunkirk and to Antwerp, Ghent and Terneuzen. The service from Liverpool was weekly and calls to Manchester varied from weekly to fortnightly. Colin Turner wrote in *Sea Breezes* in December 1982:

> The major inward cargoes were all bulk commodities. The Belgian services saw the importation of steel through Ellesmere Port, while flax and cotton waste went to Belfast. Cotton waste was both imported and exported through Manchester; the high and low grades being exported. Silver sand for the Lancashire glass-making industry was loaded at Antwerp and delivered to Liverpool. Manchester received cargoes such as starch and farina (potato starch) from France, Holland and Belgium, and strawboard, a form of cardboard, was a feature of the pre-war cargoes which emanated from Rotterdam and Amsterdam. Outward cargoes consisted mainly of manufactured goods and heavy machinery.

Under the ownership of Amalgamated Industries, four new ships had been added to the fleet of the Cork Steamship Company: the *Lestris*, *Rallus*, *Vanellus* and *Ousel*. The first ship to be built by the new owners was the *Tringa*, which was constructed in Holland and launched by the wife of one of the Dutch partners. The ships were all of the same basic design, a design that was retained well into the 1950s. They had engines and accommodation amidships, including accommodation for a handful of First Class passengers, and were between 1,500 and 1,900 tons gross. They had two holds forward and two aft which were serviced by an impressive array of derricks and deck cranes.

In June 1924 a group of unusual visitors tied up at Trafford Wharf when HMS *Velux*, HMS *Versatile*, HMS *Vimy* and other ships from the First Destroyer Flotilla

The destroyer HMS *Versatile* (1918) at Eastham, on a courtesy visit to Manchester in June 1924.

arrived preparatory to being open to inspection by the public. Visits by the navy were regular occurrences at Manchester, but this one was unusual as it involved a larger number of ships than normal.

Oil imports continued to grow after the war. The Admiralty had asked that tankers be allowed up to Barton and Mode Wheel with low flashpoint cargoes during the First World War and bulk imports quickly overtook that of oil in casks. American oil also overtook that from Russia. After the war the canal company undertook to develop a new oil dock on the Stanlow promontory, opposite Ince Marshes. This was isolated, being situated 5 miles east of Eastham Locks, and suitable for handling low flashpoint products including refined petrol. Construction started in 1919 and the dock was finally opened for business in June 1922. A pipeline beneath the canal connected with a small tank farm to facilitate storage and distribution. The new facility was an immediate success as most of the larger tankers of the day could come up the canal to use it. Both Shell and Anglo-American focussed their imports on Stanlow, which by 1928 was second only to London.

It was also recognised that tankers were getting bigger and of deeper draught, so another construction phase began with the dredging of the channel to Stanlow to increase its depth from 28 feet to 30 feet, that is, to the same depth as the lock sill at Eastham. The large lock at Eastham is wider than the inland ones, being some 600 feet long and 80 feet wide. The dredging was authorised in 1924 and completed in 1926. Some tankers still went up to Barton and Mode Wheel, all having to go up to Manchester to be turned before coming down the canal again, whereas tankers could be turned off the dock at Stanlow. Anglo-American used Barton from 1920. Shell-Mex opened a small refinery plant at Stanlow in 1924 – the start of bigger things yet to come.

Eagle Oil Transport Company's tanker *San Zeferino* (1914), outbound beneath the Runcorn Transporter Bridge having unloaded at Barton. She was 420 feet long by 55 feet breadth.

The *Lord Stalbridge* (1909) was one of three passenger-carrying tugs that came into canal company ownership in 1922.

In 1922 the canal company acquired three passenger tugs previously used by the Shropshire Union Canal & Railway to tow barges between Ellesmere Port and Liverpool. The assets of the canal were split, the tugs and barges coming to the Manchester Ship Canal while the railway ultimately became part of the London Midland & Scottish Railway. The big tugs were the *Ralph Brocklebank*, dating from 1909; the *W E Dorrington*, built in 1906; and the *Lord Stalbridge*, which had been completed at Dublin in 1909. On coming into canal service, she was found to be difficult to handle and the skipper of the *Lord Stalbridge* for ten years, Captain Kortens, noted many years later that 'in a wind she needed a tug to keep her head up'!

Chapter 7

Overcoming Difficult Times: Mid-1920s to Mid-1930s

From the early hours of Tuesday 3 May 1926, some 2 million workers went on strike across Britain. The General Strike had begun. The strike was called by the Trades Union Congress in support of striking coal miners in the north of England, Scotland and Wales. The miners were making a stand against an enforced pay cut. It was the latest in a long series of industrial disputes that had dogged the coal industry since the end of the First World War and created real hardship for mining families. 'Not a minute on the day, not a penny off the pay' was the miners' slogan. The strike was symptomatic of rising costs and static wages, and more and more families had found it hard to make ends meet. The effect on the shipping industry was profound: no coal to export, no bunkers for the ships, reduced output of export goods, and reduction in trade generally.

Worse was to come. The Wall Street Crash was the United States' stock market crash of 29 October 1929, which precipitated a worldwide collapse in share values and triggered the Great Depression – years of economic slump with catastrophic levels of unemployment across the industrialised world other than the Soviet Union. Times were indeed difficult. However, a number of economists have since reported that the Port of Manchester helped to buffer the recession in the north-west of England.

The problems endured by Manchester Liners were symptomatic of the poor trading conditions between the mid-1920s and the mid-1930s. Having taken delivery of the *Manchester Commerce* and *Manchester Citizen* in 1925, the last triple-expansion engine ships built for the company, it was a further ten years before the next new ship was delivered. All were innovative, at least for Manchester Liners. The '*Commerce* and '*Citizen* were arranged to burn either coal or oil, the latter option allowing the ships to avoid bunkering difficulties during the Coal Strike in 1926.

The *Manchester Spinner* and *Manchester Civilian*, both slow ships with a speed of just 10 knots, had been on charter to the Dominion Coal Company of Sydney, Nova Scotia, on coastal collier duties to ports in the St Lawrence since the early 1920s. On top of the coal they generally carried a layer of iron ore, both very dirty cargoes. In 1931 the '*Spinner* returned to Manchester to lay up and her coaly consort followed her shortly afterwards. The steamers were laid up because the charter rates no longer covered the costs of operating the vessels. However, the *Manchester Spinner* returned to Dominion Coal for several extended periods in the 1930s, finally coming off charter in November 1938, operational at cost being favourable to the price of an idle ship. The big steamer *Manchester Regiment* fared little better and generally only came out of hibernation for the autumn grain season; her holds were otherwise far too big for the trade on offer. The *Manchester Regiment* was laid up at Manchester for the last time between March and October 1935, after which she found continuous employment on her owner's Atlantic trades. Other ships in the fleet were laid up from time to time while some of the older ships were sold at low prices. One, the *Manchester Corporation*, was sold for scrap in 1929, returning just a few thousand pounds for the value of her metal.

A ship that could not come up to Manchester was the reefer *El Argentino*, which was jointly owned on a 50/50 basis by Manchester Liners and the British & Argentine Steam Navigation Company (Houlder Brothers). The old refrigerated steamer *Manchester City* had served her time, maintaining the River Plate service and running also to the St Lawrence, as required, to load Canadian beef and dairy products. *Manchester Liners – An Extraordinary Story* reports:

> While Manchester Liners was reluctant to commit itself to a new build for the River Plate service, an opportunity arose which offered a good compromise. The British & Argentine Steam Navigation Company, which was managed by Furness owned Houlder Brothers, was building a large new refrigerated motor ship at the Fairfield Shipbuilding & Engineering Company yard at Govan. She was 431 feet long and 64.5 feet broad, and her loaded draught prevented her from ever using the Manchester

The *El Argentino* (1928) was half owned by Manchester Liners but had too deep a draught ever to come up to Manchester. (John Clarkson)

Ship Canal. Her engines were twin six cylinder Sulzer oil engines driving separate shafts and built under license at Fairfield and these were to provide a service speed of over 14 knots. The Manchester Liners Board was able to negotiate a half share in the new ship which cost a total of £412,000 to complete. Manchester Liners parted with a cheque for £206,000 and became the proud owners of half a motor ship.

The *El Argentino* had a deadweight of 10,100 tons with a draught of 31 feet. She had an impressive 557,000 cubic feet of refrigerated space divided between fifty-two chambers. There was also comfortable accommodation for twelve passengers. The ship returned the original investment to Manchester Liners several times over.

In 1930 a long-standing ban on importing live cattle from Canada was lifted. However, almost at the same time the Salford lairage was closed so that inbound ships had to call at the Birkenhead lairage to disembark cattle. Manchester Liners only survived the recession because it had prepared for the worst. It had reduced its product to the core Canadian service, having retrenched from Philadelphia in the 1920s, and it had sold and laid up ships as a prudent measure in the face of hard times. Other companies working out of Manchester were not as well placed and fared much worse, some of the tramp companies being hardest hit. At the worst point about one-third of the merchant ships registered in Britain were laid up, their crews at home with no income, their owners covering the costs of the lay-up.

Frederick Leyland & Company continued to send ships up to Manchester, generally from Boston and occasionally also from New York. The Manchester visit was by inducement, but the company's big cargo liners were regularly to be seen in No. 8 Dock. Six intermediate-sized cargo liners had been delivered immediately after the First World War, the *Barbadian*, *Belgian*, *Bolivian* of 5,300 tons gross and the *Philadelphian*, *Dakarian* and *Norwegian* of 6,500 tons gross. The recession hit the company very hard, however, and in the early 1930s a number of its ships were laid up both at Manchester and at Liverpool. In 1932 the International Mercantile Marine Company sold its interests in the Leyland Line and as a consequence the fleet was disposed of piecemeal, the more modern ships seeing further trading for new owners. The pink and black-topped funnels of the Leyland fleet were seen no more.

But there was also the good news story of oil imports at Manchester. Cory Brothers moved into Barton in 1926, and the Texas Oil Company in 1928, for the import of refined products. Stanlow overtook Barton and Mode Wheel in terms of storage capacity in 1928. Shell became the dominant company at Stanlow, where the main import was petrol and oil as well as crude oil for refining. Refining started on the site when Shell-Mex opened a small plant in 1924 to deal with crude oil imported from Mexico. Lobitos Oilfields opened a larger refinery in 1934 and Anglo-American in 1938. Refined petrol started to become a significant export from the canal during the late 1920s.

In 1931, work on a second large oil dock was commenced alongside what now became known as Stanlow No. 1 Dock. No. 2 Dock was opened on 26 May 1933, with Alexander Towing Company's excursion ship *Ryde*, formerly the White Star Line tender *Magnetic*, attending with invited guests. During the opening ceremony the

BP tanker *British Duchess* came up from Eastham and berthed in the new dock. The *British Duchess* was a 6,000-ton tanker built in 1924. She was 405 feet long by 55 feet broad, drawing 28 feet of water fully loaded, but still leaving plenty of room in the lock at Eastham and with two feet of water beneath her keel. The tanker sailed in ballast for Alexandria on 25 May.

Another good news story was the new Furness Pacific service via the Panama Canal to the west coast of America and Canada. Between 1927 and 1929 seven new Pacific ships were delivered, so that the Manchester to Vancouver service could be upgraded to fortnightly. Interestingly, these ships all had twin engines and twin screws that gave them an extra knot over the earlier ships, and a cruising speed of 12½ knots. The ships also illustrate how cargo liners were growing in dimensions on the long-haul services. The *Pacific Trader* and *Pacific Shipper* delivered for the service in 1924 were 420 feet long by 58 feet breadth, whereas the *Pacific Enterprise* class (the *Pacific Enterprise*, *'Exporter*, *'Reliance 'Pioneer* and *'Ranger*), which started to be delivered from 1927 onwards, were 436 feet long with a beam of 60 feet and the *Pacific Grove* and *Pacific President*, delivered in 1928, were 450 feet long by 61 feet breadth.

Most of the ships on the Pacific service were registered under the ownership of the Norfolk & North American Steamship Company, although the *'Trader*, *'President* and *'Grove* were owned by parent Furness Withy & Company. Following the Wall Street Crash the service remained as before and continued to run at fortnightly intervals, although loadings outbound were light. Some sailings terminated at Liverpool during the depression, it not being worthwhile to make the transit up the ship canal with the cargoes available. The buoyancy of the imports reflected the range of western seaboard ports called at and the variety of goods available for import.

A number of shipowners were introduced to Manchester during the First World War. Finding no ill effects from the experience, they continued to use Manchester as merchants and cargoes demanded. These included the Royal Mail Line, Pacific Steam Navigation Company and the Harrison Line, whose ships were increasingly seen in the canal. However, many other companies steadfastly refused even to consider Manchester as an option.

On 18 June 1929, another notable visit by the Royal Navy to Manchester was made when five members of the Sixth Destroyer Flotilla arrived at Trafford Wharf. The fleet comprised four W Class destroyers, HMS *Wakeful*, HMS *Wessex*, HMS *Westcott* and HMS *Wolfhound*, plus the Scott Class flotilla leader HMS *Campbell*. The ships were open to the public during their week-long stay and proved an immense attraction, with crowds queuing up from Trafford Road Bridge and along Trafford Road. Manchester Corporation fêted the crews, who were offered trips to Belle Vue Zoological Gardens (and amusement park) and to Blackpool.

An announcement was made in the Australian press in September 1932 to the effect that:

Following representations made recently by leading Manchester importers and other business interests, a direct shipping service between Australia and the Port of Manchester will be inaugurated next month. A vessel will leave once a month. The

Harrison Line's *Senator* (1917) outbound below Mode Wheel Lock with the stern paddle tug *Rixton* (1907).

Harrison's *Author* (1914) seen outbound at Latchford with the bow tug *Eastham* (1899); the *Author* was one of many ships to be sold for demolition during the recession.

HMS *Wessex* (1918) was one of five members of the Sixth Destroyer Flotilla to arrive at Manchester on 18 June 1929. The fleet was opened to the public and proved an immense attraction.

trade will be served by the Federal Steam Navigation Company and the Ellerman & Bucknall Line and the Scottish Shire Line.

This was a welcome return to an earlier trade, which had lapsed in the late 1920s, that enabled Australian dairy products and chilled meat to be brought directly to Manchester. Departures had tended to be reduced during the recession, with weekly services becoming fortnightly and fortnightly services becoming monthly. Some routes were abandoned altogether. These cutbacks allowed companies to thin their fleets, with many older ships going to the breakers' yards while many more modern vessels were laid up awaiting better trading conditions.

One service that failed because of the slump in America was the joint Ellerman/Lamport & Holt/White Star Line service between Manchester and New York. The route had been loss-making throughout the 1920s and Ellerman had become increasingly disillusioned with it. In 1934 it was given up and left to Lamport & Holt to maintain as best they could; White Star abandoned the joint service preparatory to its merger with Cunard, and Ellerman unsuccessfully offered its share to the Leyland Line. The last Ellerman sailing was by the *City of Derby* in January 1934.

The Ellerman service to the Mediterranean developed from the purchase of the Watson company during the First World War, now extended in competition with the Prince Line to a variety of ports in Egypt, Syria and Cyprus, and included the all-important Jaffa orange trade from the Eastern Mediterranean. The Liverpool

Ellerman's *City of Venice* (1924) working cargo at No. 8 Dock. She had accommodation for 170 passengers and was later transferred to Ellerman City Line.

service by the Ellerman-owned Papayanni Line and Ellerman's Manchester interests were finally merged as Ellerman & Papayanni Lines in 1932, allowing a weekly service during the height of the orange season.

The domestic and near Continental trades continued much as before. British & Continental Steamship Company continued to expand its routes. Five new ships were delivered to serve this expansion between 1925 and 1928, along with one ship acquired second-hand. Colin Turner explains in an article in *Sea Breezes* from December 1982:

> The first ship to be built for the British & Continental Steamship Company was the *Tringa* of 1925 (1,930 gross tons) which was constructed in Holland and launched by the wife of the chairman of P.A. van Es; a reflection of the company's extensive Dutch interests... The three sisters *Pandion*, *Dafila* and *Tadorna* averaged 1,943 gross tons and were delivered between 1926 and 1928. ... Acquired in 1926 was the Swedish Lloyd steamer *Holmia* (1,600 gross tons) which was renamed *Serula*. She had been built in 1918 and was strengthened for ice navigation.

However, two ships, the *Whimbrel* and the *Fulmar*, were lost in collisions in the rivers Scheldt and Mersey respectively, in 1926 and 1927. Eight of the older members of the fleet were then sold in the worst of the recession, the first in 1929, the last in 1933. The company itself did survive, although its services were much reduced.

The Hollandsche Stoomboot Maatschappij NV (Holland Steamship Company) operated a regular service from Amsterdam to Manchester and Liverpool with the

The *Dafila* (1928) was one of three sisters built in Scotland for the British & Continental Steamship Company. She is seen here beneath the Warburton High Level Bridge.

steamer *Texelstroom*, dating from 1918. The extension of the Amsterdam–Liverpool service up to Manchester had commenced before the First World War. The *Texelstroom* carried a few passengers and provided a ten-day cruise to Amsterdam and back for discerning clientele, a popular voyage in the summer months. Departures from Manchester were approximately every two weeks. The *Texelstroom* was usually supported as required by the steamers *Amstelstroom* or *Zaanstroom*, completed for the company in 1919 and 1920 respectively.

Fisher Renwick & Company Manchester–London Steamers continued to run their twice-weekly departure from Pomona Docks to Southampton and London. Passenger berths continued to be made available between London and Manchester but passengers could not join or leave the ship at Southampton. The ships were all registered in Manchester. The oldest member of the fleet, the *Yeoman*, dating from 1901, was sold in 1929, reducing the fleet to the *Lancer*, built in 1909; *Cuirassier* of 1914; *Sapper* of 1923; and the *Sentry*, built the following year. Other ships were brought in from time to time from the main fleet, based at Newcastle, and conversely the Manchester ships also occasionally served on the main company's North Sea trades. The Manchester–London company had started to develop road haulage interests in the early 1920s, working largely in competition with the Manchester Ship Canal's Bridgewater Department road services. Throughout the depressed years of the late 1920s and early 1930s, this side of the business was developed so that a daily lorry service was available to the Midlands and London at rates that compared favourably

The *Amstelstroom* (1919), owned by Hollandsche Stoomboot Maatschappij NV, was a regular relief steamer on the Amsterdam service. She is seen in No. 8 Dock.

with those offered by the railway companies. The steamers continued to ply between Manchester and London with the larger and heavier loads, although they lost much of the parcel service to the lorries.

In 1929 the cargo service to Belfast operated by the Belfast & Manchester Steamship Company was rebranded under the title Belfast, Mersey & Manchester Steamship Company. The Clyde Shipping Company's steamer *Saltees*, dating from 1899, was purchased for the service to Liverpool and on to Manchester. She was given the name *Stormont*. The original steamer on the Manchester route, the *Manchester* of 1891, was sold for scrap in 1933. She was replaced by the *Greypoint*, another ex-Clyde Shipping Company vessel, formerly the *Rathlin*, completed in 1903.

Coast Lines continued its twice-weekly departures for Glasgow, inherited from M. Langlands & Sons immediately after the First World War. The *Anglesey Coast* was largely dedicated to the Glasgow–Manchester cargo service while the *Ayrshire Coast*, originally designed for Langlands, regularly visited Manchester before calling at Liverpool on the return journey to Glasgow. The *Scottish Coast*, another vessel also ordered originally for Langlands, was the mainstay on the Manchester–Leith service with calls on return at Dundee, Aberdeen and Stornoway. This was extended to Middlesbrough in 1933 when the west coast terminal became Liverpool.

The Belfast services continued on a twice-weekly basis, the former Langlands cargo steamer *Lairdsbrook* becoming a regular on the Belfast run from 1930 onwards for Burns & Laird Lines, often returning via Glasgow. Belfast Steamship Company also worked between Manchester and Belfast, while British & Irish Steam Packet provided a weekly service direct to Dublin.

A noticeable difference in the shipping using the canal was a sharp increase in coastal tankers exporting refined petroleum products and chemicals. Metcalf Motor Coasters'

The *Greypoint* (1903) was a regular caller at Manchester on the Belfast route after she was acquired by the Belfast, Mersey & Manchester Steamship Company in 1933.

The *Lancashire Coast* (1920) was originally designed for Langlands and is seen at Pomona Docks on Coast Lines' Leith service, standing in for quasi-sister *Scottish Coast* (1922).

first tanker, the *Frank M*, was a regular visitor to Stanlow from her completion in 1929 onwards. F. T. Everard & Sons were increasingly active in the ship canal as they too invested in tankers during this same period. Examples included the *Alchemyst*, completed in 1895 and which served the company until 1950, and the *Audacity*, completed only in 1929. The company's dry cargo ships were less evident in the canal, although calls were occasionally made. The small tankers owned by Shell-Mex and Esso were also regular visitors to Stanlow and Barton.

United States government sponsorship of American flag shipping led to an increase in American vessels arriving at Manchester. Many ships were built by the United States Shipping Board and managed by newly formed companies that were run on commercial lines. The United States Lines Company, for example, brought the registry 'New York, NY State' on their sterns, adding colour to the city docks. A variety of other American shipping companies also visited Manchester, with ships belonging to the Waterman Steamship Company of Mobile, and to three companies of New York, the American Scantic Line (Scantic reflecting the company's trading area of Scandinavia and the Baltic), the Submarine Boat Corporation and the Sperling Steamship & Trading Company.

Tramp steamers continued to visit Manchester in increasing numbers despite the poor trading conditions. Almost invariably, they were used to import bulk cargoes such as timber, grain or minerals, or brought to the coal tips at Partington to load coal for export. The ships came in all sizes from owners registered in the great tramp shipping centre of the north-east of England and elsewhere in Britain. The change to overseas shipping was also noticeable, with foreign flag vessels bringing goods to Manchester mainly on single voyages. Ancient Russian steamers arrived at Trafford Wharf to discharge timber, returning home lightly loaded with specialist manufactured goods including engineering products, machinery and machine parts. A variety of other national flags became common sights along the canal as more and more trade was carried in foreign ships, the margins even then favouring foreign flag shipowners.

A number of interesting small tugs came into ship canal company ownership in 1926 and 1927. They were bought to replace the old Bridgewater Navigation Company's tugs used to tow barges across the Mersey to Liverpool: they were the *Earl of Ellesmere*, *Brackley*, *Dagmar* and *St Winnifred*, each built between 1857 and 1870. The new tugs were bought from the government and had been built in 1916 and 1917 by the Lytham Shipbuilding Company for use by the British Army in France. They were twin-screw ships and were highly manoeuvrable in confined spaces. They were named *HS 15* sequentially up to *HS 18* and were renamed *MSC Manchester*, *MSC Salford*, *MSC Runcorn* and *MSC Ellesmere Port* respectively on entering canal service.

A new fire tender was delivered in 1935 by Henry Robb at Leith. The powerful tug *MSC Firefly* was a replacement for the old fire tender *Firefly*, built at Greenwich for the company in 1904. The old tender had twin screws and twin boilers, one of which was always kept in steam to ensure a quick response to emergencies. The new tug-fire tender, *MSC Firefly*, was intended to be kept on harbour duties above Mode Wheel but was often pressed into general towage duties. Her firefighting equipment was constructed by Merryweather & Sons of London, famous then for the manufacture

Typical of the many American ships that started to frequent the ship canal in the 1920s was the *Conehatta* (1920), built for the US government. She was transferred to the American Scantic Line in 1929 but wrecked in November that same year near Holmsund, Sweden.

The *Saxilby* (1914) was one of the many tramp ships owned by the Ropner Shipping Company of West Hartlepool. She is seen discharging cargo at No. 9 Dock in July 1926. Sadly, she was lost with all hands in the Atlantic in November 1933 with the *Manchester Regiment* one of three ships looking for survivors.

The *Dagmar* (1863) was the last of the former Bridgewater Canal Mersey estuary tugs to be broken up when she was sold in 1927 along with the *St Winifred* (1870).

The *MSC Firefly* (1935) was a fire-fighting harbour tug intended for use above Mode Wheel but often seen on general towage duties. She replaced the original company fire tender *Firefly* (1904), built for the company at Greenwich. (Author)

of fire engines and a company that is today still very active in the field of firefighting.

The trade of the Manchester Ship Canal was slowly evolving. Whereas timber, grain and cotton had been the three most important imports by volume, although in the reverse order by value, oil had now overtaken timber and grain. Farnie wrote:

> By 1928 Stanlow ranked second only to London as a port for the import and distribution of petrol and had expanded its storage capacity above that available at the Barton-Mode Wheel end. Shell surpassed Anglo-American in storage capacity by 1929 and created a huge centre for distribution by road, rail and Ship Canal. The inflow of petroleum products developed on a large scale ... to become the largest import into the Port of Manchester.

Specially constructed oil barges were used to bring refined products up the canal from Stanlow to Mode Wheel as a secondary road-based distribution centre. Seagoing tankers also brought refined products up the canal to Mode Wheel and Barton. At Barton a new specialist refinery was under construction for the blending and refining of specialist industrial oils.

Manchester emerged from the Great Depression with a keen eye for new industrial and commercial developments. It was now recognised that far from having eroded the trade of Liverpool, the Port of Manchester had, if anything, improved the prospects of Liverpool by attracting new industries to the region and by expanding the export market. Manchester and Liverpool now tended to work together, although neither had yet learned to trust the other.

The shipping industry had been hard hit by the economic slump, but shipowners were poised to take advantage of the upturn in business. Manchester Liners was at the forefront with a new class of coal-fired, albeit with automatic stokers using pulverised coal, turbine steamer in the design office at the Blythswood Shipbuilding Company at Scotstoun on the Clyde. A contract was placed in 1934 at a price of £129,000, with an option for two further ships, resulting in the launching of the *Manchester Port* in July 1935. She arrived at Manchester in October ready for duty. Her design incorporated the carriage of live cattle, with ventilated compartments for the carriage of fruit. Accommodation was provided for twelve passengers, while the crew's quarters were said to be a great improvement on any previous ship in the fleet. Following her maiden voyage to Canada she was proclaimed such a success that an order was immediately placed for a second ship. The so-called *Manchester Port* Class was indeed a success, the last of this class of eight ships, the *Manchester Merchant*, being completed in 1951.

Chapter 8

End of the Recession –
and the Second World War

Unemployment continued to fall through 1935 and 1936. Devaluation of the pound helped to improve exports of manufactured goods. A policy of rearmament started in 1936, which in turn generated new jobs and work for the shipyards. By 1937 unemployment had fallen to 1.5 million, but by January 1938 it had risen again to 1.8 million, reflecting a slow and painful economic recovery that started in the south and slowly spread northwards. For the shipping industry the recession was followed by a decline in Britain's trading position, an increase in the use of foreign registered tonnage coupled with a need for shipowners to keep abreast of the many technical advances that were then being introduced.

On the bright side, occasional excursions between Liverpool and Manchester were resumed in 1937. The small twin-funnelled motor ship *St Silio* took her first excursion from Manchester Pomona Docks to Liverpool on Wednesday 22 September 1937, her passengers returning to Manchester by train. On this occasion she had come up the canal light but on future excursions, usually at the start and end of the summer season, she carried passengers both ways. The Liverpudlians always derided the poor ship's name, so in 1946 she was renamed *St Trillo*, the name by which she is now better remembered.

The *Port of Manchester Official Sailing List and Shipping Guide 1936* listed regular sailings to twelve ports in the British Isles and nearly 200 ports overseas, with occasional sailings to a further ninety foreign ports. It also reported some 5,000 arrivals at Eastham. The summary of the port's services read:

> … regular services with the Canadian ports, Montreal, Quebec, St John's and Halifax, USA, North Atlantic, Southern and Pacific ports; South America, inward services only from the River Plate and Brazil; South and East Africa; India inward from Calcutta and Colombo, to and from Bombay and Karachi; the Persian Gulf; Egypt and the Near East; Australia and New Zealand, Tasmania; the Baltic and Scandinavian ports; Russia; Spain and Portugal; North Africa and Morocco and the Mediterranean ports; Continental ports; French ports; Black Sea ports, and coastwise services.

The excursion ship *St Silio* (1936) loading passengers at Prince's Landing Stage, Liverpool, with one of the Isle of Man boats beyond.

By 1936 the Prince Line fleet had been reduced to only nineteen ships, but in October of that year the first of four new 2,090 gross ton sisters were completed for the Mediterranean service: three by W. Hamilton & Company of Port Glasgow, the *Arabian Prince*, *Palestinian Prince* and *Syrian Prince*, and one, a new *Cyprian Prince*, by the Furness Shipbuilding Company at Haverton Hill. The company was given a 100 per cent government loan of £130,000 for the construction of the *Arabian Prince* and the *Syrian Prince* on the condition that two ships were scrapped under the Scrap and Build Bill. Consequently, the *Sailor Prince* and the *Stuart Prince* were sent to the scrapyard. The new ships had a single triple steam expansion engine which gave them a speed of just under 12 knots. They were attractive looking ships with an almost yacht-like appearance and had a deadweight of 2,900 tons distributed in two holds forward and one aft on a draught of 19 feet. There was First Class accommodation for a handful of passengers, who had an observation lounge on the boat deck directly beneath the bridge.

In 1939, the Mediterranean fleet consisted of the *Sicilian Prince*, *Sardinian Prince*, *Egyptian Prince*, *Arabian Prince*, *Palestinian Prince*, a new *Cyprian Prince* and *Syrian Prince*. The last four were coal-burning ships. Just before the Second World War, Prince Line ordered four new ships for the Mediterranean service; the *Norman Prince*, *Tudor Prince* and *Stuart Prince* were delivered in 1940, followed by the *Lancastrian Prince* in 1941. All four were requisitioned for government service and only the *Tudor Prince* and *Stuart Prince* survived to take up civilian duties after the war. The *Italian Prince*, which was built for Furness Withy as the *Italiana* in 1922, had been lost when she caught fire off Finisterre on passage to Alexandretta on 6 September 1938. The fire broke out in the boiler room, but as it could not be controlled and as the ship had a deck cargo of detonators in a magazine stowed on deck, the passengers and crew evacuated the ship as the fire took hold.

Two more ships of the *Manchester Port* Class joined the Manchester Liners fleet. These were the *Manchester City*, named in honour of the 1936/37 First Division Championship win of the local football team, and the *Manchester Progress*, which was launched in June 1938. Like the earlier *Manchester Port,* they were coal-burners with automatic stokers using pulverised coal. This was a system clearly favoured over that of the oil-burners, *Manchester Commerce* and *Manchester Citizen*, completed in 1925, despite the success of these ships. Bunkers for them were available at Stanlow prior to departure. The *Manchester Merchant* was the next of the turbine ships to be delivered, arriving in Manchester in April 1940 adorned in camouflage grey, followed almost a year later by the *Manchester Trader*. Then the first oil-burner of the class finally appeared, the *Manchester Shipper*, which was delivered in October 1943.

The *Manchester Shipper* was fitted up with temporary accommodation for seventy-five passengers in the shelter deck, there being considerable demand from military personnel for transatlantic travel. The Ministry of War Transport also converted the three Harrison Line ships *Advisor*, *Settler* and *Strategist* to carry sixty passengers in accommodation described as 'of a rather primitive nature'. In all cases the accommodation was removed after the war and the ships reverted to their cargo liner duties. The *Settler* Class was the last to be delivered to the Harrison Line before the war. They were two-decked ships of about 9,000 tons deadweight, with a triple-expansion engine coupled to a low pressure turbine with double reduction gearing and hydraulic coupling.

In 1938 even the piece goods trade to India had improved such that the Manchester Chamber of Commerce and the Bradford Chamber signed an agreement for sole shipping with the Conference lines, i.e. City Line, Hall and W. Tither to Karachi and in addition the Clan and Anchor lines to Bombay. Clan Line ships also visited Manchester inbound with cargoes such as grain from Australia.

A new Guinness boat had been delivered in 1931 for the sixty-hour run between Dublin and London. However, once the new Park Royal Brewery opened in London in 1938 the ship was transferred to the Manchester route, berth to berth normally carried out in just nineteen hours. The new ship was aptly named the *Guinness*. She carried 800 tons of stout in large casks in a single large hold which she unloaded at the Guinness store in Pomona Docks, loading empties topped with large sacks of barley for the main brewery in Dublin on the return trip. She was supported in this role by the former colliers *Carrowdore* and *Clarecastle*, the latter pair also running to Garston. The import of stout from Ireland continued throughout the war that followed, it being considered an important morale booster. The ships, being Dublin registered, were in any case neutral.

Fisher Renwick sold their shipping interests and their three remaining steamers, *Cuirassier*, *Sapper* and *Sentry*, to Coast Lines in 1939. The fourth ship in the fleet, the *Lancer*, had been sold in 1937 to the Stanhope Steamship Company, which gave

The *Italian Prince* (1922) was one of three new ships transferred from Furness Withy to the Prince Line in 1922. She was lost in 1938, on fire off Finisterre.

The *Manchester Commerce* (1925) at Barton. Note the stern paddle tug is going astern to increase the flow of water over the liner's rudder and hence increase the ship's sensitivity to the helm. (Manchester Ship Canal Company)

The *Manchester Shipper* (1943), built under licence as a replacement for the *Manchester Merchant* (1941). The *Manchester Shipper* is seen at peace towards the end of her career; she is heading up the canal below Barton Locks in September 1967. (Author)

The *Guinness* (1931) started running between Dublin and the Guinness store at Pomona Docks in 1938 when she was no longer needed on the Dublin to London route. (Author)

her the name *Stanbrook*. Thereafter, the service between Manchester and London was downgraded to weekly with occasional extra sailings to Southampton. Under Coast Lines ownership, the *Cuirassier* became the *Thames Coast*, the *Sapper* the *Avon Coast* and the *Sentry* the *Medway Coast*. Until the outbreak of war the three ships were kept on Manchester–London duties by Coast Lines; however, the service was only operated on an ad hoc basis thereafter.

That was not the end of Fisher Renwick – but rather a new start. The company focussed on its road haulage interests. It had introduced the first Scammell articulated lorries and it pioneered road transport with the introduction of its 'Continuous Service' using Scammell vans and flatbed lorries. In the late 1940s Fisher Renwick again changed its focus to become a leading supplier of contract hire vehicles; later in 1972 it was acquired by truck rental and logistics company Ryder.

The CWS service between Rouen and Manchester maintained by the *CWS Progress* ended in 1937. Sailings had been on Friday afternoons, calling at Swansea on the way out. The reason given for the closure was that the introduction of the forty-hour working week in France necessitated savings to be made and the cutting of the Manchester service was seen as a suitable way of compensating.

The first of a series of twin-screw motor tugs took up duty on the canal in 1940, as W. B. Hallam reported in *Sea Breezes* in June 1968:

> The development of oil-engined tugs attracted the attention of the [Ship Canal] company in 1939, and the suitability of motor tugs for work along the Canal with its stringent requirements for safety and reliability was investigated. As a result an order was placed with Henry Robb for four motor tugs which came to the waterway in 1940-1942. The *MSC Mallard* and *MSC Merlin* were delivered in 1940, the *MSC Neptune* in 1941 being followed in 1942 by the *MSC Nymph*. These tugs are of 131 tons gross, powered by Crossley engines [manufactured in Manchester] developing 770 brake horse power, driving twin screws.

On 26 August 1939 Whitehall issued an order that stated that the Cabinet committee responsible for 'defence preparedness' had authorised the Admiralty to adopt compulsory control of all movements of merchant shipping. The Admiralty took charge of each ship as it completed its peacetime duties, assuming full control once it had discharged its cargo, wherever it was around the world. Of course, this took some time to accomplish, but thereafter the responsibility for loading and unloading became that of the Ministry of Shipping (renamed the Ministry of War Transport in 1941) and not the shipowner. A great deal of planning had been carried out once the newly formed Ministry of Shipping had been set up. Owners already knew which of their ships would be requisitioned and which would receive guns as Defensively Armed Merchant Ships. Indeed, some ships had already been stiffened ready to take the gun mounting.

It had also been agreed that the convoy system would be adopted again. Convoys were much hated by seafarers, who felt trapped inside them; disliked by the Air Force, who considered that a single ship was a more difficult target to hit in an air strike; and subject to a general belief that submarines would not be deployed by the Germans as

The compact engine room aboard *MSC Mallard* (1940) with the two Crossley diesels on either side.

First of a new class of motor tugs was the *MSC Mallard* (1940), built by Henry Robb of Leith complete with two Manchester-built Crossley oil engines developing 770 horsepower. (Author)

they were in the First World War as it was the submarine that finally brought America into that war. Transatlantic convoys, however, were to be poorly defended once they were 200 miles beyond the most westerly shore base at Londonderry, at which point the escort vessels had to return home. Britain had only given up its two naval stations on the west coast of the Irish Free State in 1938.

War was declared on Sunday 3 September 1939. During the course of the year, when war had seemed an inevitability, the Furness Pacific fleet was heavily involved with importing American-built military aircraft, as David Burrell reports in his history of Furness Withy:

> By early 1939 they all carried sealed Admiralty orders, to be opened on the outbreak of war. The ships on the North Pacific service carried an even more obvious sign, aircraft stowed on deck for the passage to England. Some of the ships even had their lifeboats swung out to enable extra aircraft to be secured on the boat decks. Devised by the Los Angeles office of Furness Withy a method of deck stowage was perfected and about seven aircraft could be carried on deck making the best possible use of the space available.

Manchester again felt vulnerable to attack, but the key objective of the enemy – to maim one of the five sets of locks that enabled the Port of Manchester – was fortunately never achieved. Bombing raids on Trafford Park and on the dock estate were carried out throughout 1940. The tall wooden structure of the No. 1 Grain Elevator was hit by an incendiary bomb; it did not take long to ignite, burning and smouldering for several weeks before it collapsed onto Trafford Wharf. The fire brigade had worried about the fire hazard that the structure posed ever since it was completed in 1898 and were not sorry to see it go.

Stanlow became critical to the war effort and again the plant and its berths were largely undamaged by enemy action during the war. Farnie wrote in his economic history of the Port of Manchester:

> During the war ... Stanlow was integrated into a new national system of transportation, being linked by pipeline to Bromborough in 1941, to Avonmouth in 1942 and by a great quadrilateral line to Misterton, Sandy and Aldermaston in 1943, so becoming with Avonmouth one of the twin sources of supply of aviation fuel to the airfields of Eastern England.

At night, ships in convoy were blacked out and manoeuvres had to be accurate to avoid collisions. On the night of 4 December 1939 two regular Manchester ships, the *Chancellor* and the *Manchester Regiment*, were lost in the blackout in the same convoy. South-west of Cape Race in a westbound convoy, Harrison Line's *Chancellor* and the Athel tanker *Athelchief* collided in the dark. The *Chancellor* was badly holed and started sinking, while the tanker, with her numerous cargo bulkheads, remained buoyant. The Pacific Steam Navigation Company's big troopship *Oropesa* was instructed to return to where the *Chancellor* had sunk in order to pick up survivors. Having successfully completed her lifesaving task, the *Oropesa* set about returning to the safety of the convoy. As she did so she collided with the *Manchester Regiment*, which was on passage from Manchester to St John, New Brunswick. The *Manchester Regiment*, one time flagship of Manchester Liners, was hastily abandoned and sank quickly, taking nine of the ship's company with her.

The new turbine steamer *Manchester Merchant* was sunk with the loss of thirty-six men out of a total complement of sixty-seven in February 1943 while on passage from Manchester to Halifax. The licence to build the *Manchester Shipper* was issued after this loss.

At their home port, ships belonging to Manchester Liners were handed over to the shore gang while their seagoing crews spent time ashore with their families. At night-time the ships were completely shut down and left to a watchman stationed at the head of the gangway with only an oil light for company. In the blackout he had not even that; a scary prospect once the air raid warning had sounded.

During 1940, three ships belonging to the Furness Pacific fleet, *Pacific Pioneer*, *Pacific President* and *Pacific Shipper*, were involved in taking gold bullion and transferable shares from England to the United States. The ships each took a single consignment worth £3 million. Manchester Liners were also responsible for transporting £25 million in eight consignments while Prince Line ships took a further £20 million. The gold and the transferable shares included Dutch, Belgian and French bullion previously shipped

The dining saloon aboard the hapless *Manchester Regiment* (1922), where all twelve passengers once sat in the style of the traditional long table.

to Britain for safekeeping, while Britain realised that if Nazi Germany was not to get hold of it all then it needed to be sent on to America. It was also a sound policy in that it could be exchanged there for war materials and stores including ships and aircraft.

The Furness Pacific ships did not fare well in the war. The *Pacific Reliance* was sunk by torpedo off the Longships on 4 March 1940 while on passage from London to Liverpool to complete discharge of cargo from the North Pacific. The *Pacific Ranger* was torpedoed on 12 October the same year while homeward bound from Seattle, followed on 2 December by the *Pacific President* with the loss of the complete complement of fifty-two that were aboard. Fortunately, all the crews of the *Pacific Reliance* and *Pacific Ranger* survived. In July 1942 the *Pacific Pioneer* was lost to a torpedo fired from a submarine, followed by the *Pacific Grove* in April 1943. Only the *Pacific Shipper*, *Pacific Enterprise* and *Pacific Exporter* survived the war. The former consort of the *Pacific Shipper*, the *Pacific Trader*, had been sold in 1937.

The invasion by Germany of the Low Countries on 10 May 1940 caused the loss of the British & Continental steamer *Tringa*. She had been able to get away from Antwerp in time to avoid capture but hit a mine on the voyage home, sinking shortly afterwards with the loss of seventeen men. The *Dotterel* did make it home to Manchester, as Colin Turner wrote in *Sea Breezes* in December 1982:

She was lying at Rotterdam when the invasion commenced, having been ordered there from Antwerp, at which port she had arrived on 3 May with a cargo of steel from

The *Pacific Exporter* (1928) carried a crew of fifty on the run between Manchester and the Pacific coast of North America.

Manchester. She, like the other vessels caught in the port, shared the bombing and strafing which Rotterdam was receiving. The situation looked very bad, as the river seemed to have been blocked when, as the first attacks had been taking place, a partially completed ship had been launched into the river from one of the shipyards ...

The *Dotterel* successfully negotiated the obstruction in the channel and steamed down the river with orders to proceed to Ijmuiden, where a large number of refugees had gathered. Despite constant attention from enemy aircraft, the *Dotterel* was got alongside the quay and over the next 24 hours every available space was filled with refugees. Included in her 'passenger list' were British families, a war correspondent, air crews and a contingent of the Sadlers Wells ballet. A valuable consignment of diamonds was also given into Captain Green's care. The *Dotterel* was equipped with degaussing gear and this enabled her to avoid the *Tringa*'s fate. She proceeded to Manchester after landing her passengers at Harwich.

In May 1940, a new shipping enterprise was established with the approval of the Ministry of Shipping to trade from Canada to Manchester, London or occasionally the Clyde Emergency Port. The Newsprint Supply Company was set up by the newspaper proprietors to buy newsprint in Canada and ship it to England for sale to the newspapers. The proprietors were nervous that 'non-essential' newsprint supplies would otherwise dry up and their businesses be put at risk. Two American ships were bought in August, the *Barberrys* and the *Pachesham*, and registered under the ownership of the Barberrys Steamship Company and the Pachesham Steamship

Company. Management of the ships was vested with Runciman (London). The two companies immediately placed orders for single ships and in 1943 the *Kelmscott* and *Caxton* were delivered. By then the *Barberrys* had already been sunk by torpedo with heavy loss of life and a number of chartered ships had also been lost. The *Kelmscott* was also hit by a torpedo, but she was towed safely to St John's and later taken to Baltimore for repairs.

The Christmas Blitz in 1940 was a devastating blow to Manchester and Trafford Park, although the Dock Estate got away relatively lightly. At 5.15 p.m. on Sunday 22 December 1940, 270 German aircraft crossed the English coast, bound for Manchester. Two waves of bombing, from 7.45 p.m. to 1.20 a.m. and from 2 a.m. to 6.55 a.m., concentrated first on Manchester city centre, then the docks and industrial areas of Salford and Trafford Park. The next evening 170 more planes arrived over Manchester. That night, the Luftwaffe hit the Metropolitan-Vickers factory in Trafford Park and thirteen partly built bombers were destroyed. Luftwaffe target maps identify the meat storage depot at Trafford Park, two sites on the pier between Nos 8 and 9 docks, two nearer Trafford Road and two on the north bank of Pomona Docks, while the lock gates at Mode Wheel were seemingly not a priority target.

During the Christmas Blitz one of the aerial mines fell onto the tug-fire tender *MSC Firefly* and penetrated into the deck locker alongside the engine room without exploding. Sub-Lieutenant Brooke-Smith arrived to deal with it and found that the bomb was firmly wedged. Lying on the sloping engine casing, head downwards, he managed to defuse it by torchlight. Brooke-Smith was later awarded the George Cross. During the Blitz there were numerous such acts of bravery, many not recorded, by men and women who were called to act way beyond their normal line of duty.

Manchester City Corporation's first sewage sludge carrier, *Mancunium*, was mined and sunk in January 1941 at a point 2 miles north-east of the Bar lightship. She had been built in 1933 by Ferguson Brothers at Port Glasgow. For the remainder of the war, the disposal of Manchester and Salford's sewage sludge to sea was left in the hands of Salford Corporation's *Salford City*. A new *Mancunium* was launched by Ferguson in October 1946. Salford had been disposing sludge to sea since 1895 (see Chapter 4), whereas Manchester City Corporation started the practice on its own account relatively late, in 1933.

During 1940 a major programme of shipbuilding to standard designs commenced on both sides of the Atlantic. The American-built Liberty ships, equipped with a single triple steam expansion engine, and good for 11 knots, soon started to visit the canal. The faster steam turbine and oil-engined Victory ships, including the C1, C2 and C3 types, had too great an air draught to come up to Manchester, unless, as was the case with one or two of them after the war, they were modified. The Victory ships were designed in 1943 as the successor to the Liberty ships. They were built for post-war commercial use whereas the Liberty ships were intended to bolster the war effort with little prospect of commercial use in peacetime.

There were also the Ocean Class, built in the United States, with the first keel, the *Ocean Vanguard*, laid on 14 April 1941; the Canadian-built Forts, the first of which was *Fort Ville Marie*, better known after the war as the Brocklebank Line's *Makalla*;

and the Canadian Maritime Commission's Parks – the latter to a variety of designs, both dry cargo and tankers. Three of the dry cargo ships, *Westwood Park*, *Riverdale Park* and *Belwoods Park*, were managed by Manchester Liners during the war. The North Sands-type *Dentonia Park* was completed by United Shipyards in 1944 and later became one of over twenty Park ships to be owned by the Counties Ship Management Company of London; the *Dentonia Park* was renamed *Cedar Hill*. Finally there were the various classes of Empire ships built in British yards, including tramp ship designs, cargo liners, heavy lift ships, a variety of tankers and coastal tankers, colliers and tugs. Many of the coastal ships ended up after the war under the Red Ensign and F. T. Everard, for example, bought quite a few of these ships; the *Argosity*, completed in 1941 as *Empire Lass*, was one such.

The pressures of wartime on the Manchester docks system were intense. Manchester dry docks had to cope with damaged ships queuing up for repair; the ships were put back onto the high seas with the minimum of work that made them once again seaworthy. The docks themselves were intensely used, with ships lined up along Trafford Wharf for a berth in the docks on the north side. As many of the shoreside men had gone to fight the war, the residual dock labour force was inadequate for the steady stream of work needed to be carried out and turnaround times were generally extensive. Coaling of outbound vessels was carried out at Ellesmere Port to relieve pressure at Partington.

Among the heavier losses of life, whose last contact with land was at Eastham, was that of the Harrison Line's *Designer*, dating from 1928. She sailed from Manchester bound for Cape Town with military stores and the mail. On 6 July 1941 her convoy was dispersed and she headed south, but in the early hours of 9 July, in a position to the north-north-west of the Azores, the *Designer* was hit by one of two torpedoes fired from a U-boat. She sank after six minutes. The master, Captain Donald McCallum, and sixty-six crew members were lost. Tragic too was the loss of the *Lancastrian Prince*, which had sailed from Manchester in ballast bound for Boston, when on 12 April 1943 she was hit by a torpedo and sank with the loss of all thirty-seven crew members and seven gunners. The fate of the *Manchester Brigade* was equally awful, lost to a torpedo while in convoy on passage from Manchester to Montreal on 26 September 1940. There were just four survivors.

A regular caller at Ellesmere Port with Canadian pulp and paper products for Bowater's Ellesmere Port Paper Mill was the *Humber Arm*, owned by Bowater's Newfoundland Pulp & Paper Mills. Loaded with newsprint, pulp, lumber and steel, she was torpedoed in an eastbound convoy, but this time all crew were safely landed ashore. Similarly, the loss of the Harrison ship *Scholar* on 22 September 1940 incurred no loss of life. She was bound from Galveston via Halifax to Manchester. The ship was actually taken in tow for a while, having caught fire after a torpedo hit her. The tow was later abandoned and the *Scholar* was scuttled. Her manifest read: 5,484 bales of cotton, 2,023 tons of steel, 54 tons of arsenic, 242 tons of wood pulp and 965 tons of lumber.

When the news of the German surrender filtered through, and the war in Europe was finally over, the noise from the docks was tumultuous. Every ship that had steam

EXAMPLES OF WARTIME STANDARD SHIPS

Above: The *Scholar* (1945) was a typical Liberty ship, completed as the *Samidway*. She came into Harrison Line ownership in 1947 and as the *Scholar* was a regular visitor to Manchester. She is seen here at Birkenhead. (Author)

Below: Blue Funnel Line's *Mentor* (1945) was a typical C2 type Victory ship, completed as the *Carthage Victory*. Blue Funnel did not trade to Manchester and the *Mentor* could not have come up the canal without her air draught being modified. She is seen manoeuvring in Gladstone Dock, Liverpool. (Author)

Opposite above: Brocklebank's *Makalla* (1941) was the very first Canadian North Sands type standard ship to be completed. She was built by Canadian Vickers in just 300 days and was originally named *Fort Ville Marie*. She is seen here as the *Makalla* above Barton on the way up to Manchester. (Author)

Opposite middle: The *Cedar Hill* (1944) was built as the *Dentonia Park* for the Park Steamship Company and was sold by the Canadian government to the British government in 1946, joining Halifax Overseas Freighters in 1950 and Counties Ship Management in 1964. She is seen here at Irwell Park Wharf, Eccles, in April 1965, fifteen months before she was sold to be broken up. (Author)

Opposite below: The Empire Cadet-class standard coastal tanker *Empire Lass* (1941) worked for Esso as *Esso Juniata* between 1946 and 1956 and was then sold to F. T. Everard & Sons and renamed *Argosity*. As the *Argosity*, she is seen at the Barton Layby Berth in May 1961. (Author)

Harrison Line's *Scholar* (1922) during peacetime at the masting crane layby at Eastham, minus her top masts. She was sunk by torpedo on passage from Halifax to Manchester with no loss of life in September 1940.

up sounded its whistle, every factory did the same, and the noise could be heard all over the city. It was a noise both of triumphant excitement and relief, and of a new start. In peacetime, every New Year's Eve the ships would sound their whistles at midnight for a minute or two to celebrate the incoming year. On a crisp night with a north-westerly wind, they were clearly discernible in Withington and Didsbury as a reassurance that the world was all right. But on 8 May 1945 the noise was more important than that – it was a noise to which every citizen in earshot rallied and which every citizen understood. The war with Japan, however, continued.

Chapter 9

After the War was Over

War has always been one way of ending recession. But the immediate period following war is characterised by austerity and inadequate availability of labour and materials. The need to rebuild is key to getting people back to work, but this can only be done slowly as resources become available. The nation fell into limbo as people tried to get back to normal after the excitement of VE Day, despite the war with Japan continuing until 2 September. The wartime shortages persisted well into the 1950s, with ration cards issued for various foodstuffs, including sweets as well as for clothing.

The change from 'under Admiralty orders' to 'Civvy Street' did not happen overnight. Men were demobbed as and when they could be and ships were returned to their owners once their final wartime assignments were complete. Those merchant ships that had been requisitioned and converted for military duties needed dockyard attention before they could resume commercial work. Besides, the ships had all been driven hard in the war and all needed attention of some sort or another to bring them up to an acceptable standard for trade. The grey camouflage paint needed also to be overpainted with company colours and the guns and gun mountings removed. All this took time and it was not uncommon for ships still to be trading in wartime grey into 1946 and 1947.

The shipping companies also had to pick themselves up and plan for growth. The assumption had to be that the shortages would only be overcome by the redevelopment of commerce. But there was also the memory of the brief boom years after the First World War when only eighteen months of prosperity ended when the freight market collapsed in the summer of 1920. As it happened, this time the world would enjoy fifteen years of good trading conditions before the freight market changed.

In the first instance, the shipowners had to get replacement ships for those vessels lost in the war as soon as they could. New ships would allow them to resume services at regular advertised frequencies. The cost of building ships had rocketed since the late 1930s due to the high demand for new builds during the war caused by a shortage of vessels. Second-hand ships were equally inflated in price, a good time to sell but not to buy. An option favoured by many shipowners was the purchase of the surplus wartime standard ships that continued to be delivered into 1946. The Liberty ships had been built with a short lifetime in mind so they were basic tramp type steamers with triple expansion engines and a design speed of 11 knots. The cargo handling gear was basic and the forward mast just a stump. Obviously, purchase of such ships required considerable modification for them to become satisfactory in a liner trade.

Perhaps the hardest-hit liner company working out of Manchester was Furness Pacific. They came through the war with only the *Pacific Shipper*, *Pacific Enterprise* and *Pacific Exporter*, having lost five ships during the hostilities. During 1947, Furness Pacific bid for five surplus wartime standard ships; four of them were the slow, 11 knot, steam reciprocating engined Liberty ships *Samalia*, *Samavon*, *Samdaring* and *Samtredy*, which respectively adopted the names *Pacific Liberty*, *Pacific Nomad*, *Pacific Ranger* and *Pacific Importer*. The 'Sam' prefix denotes ships bought from America by the British Ministry of War Transport, which was then charged with selling them after the war. The contract price for the purchase by Furness Pacific amounted to US $544,506 for each ship. The fifth ship was the faster steam turbine powered Victory ship *Tusculum Victory*, which was renamed *Pacific Stronghold*. Faster and therefore more suitable for the Pacific coast run she might have been but, as built, her air draught prevented her – and any of the Victory ships – from going up the Manchester Ship Canal. Modifications were carried out to her before she entered service with Furness Pacific so that she received telescopic topmasts set into the crosstrees, which in turn were reduced in elevation from the deck. She also had a new shorter funnel. As such she was one of only a very few Victory ships which were altered in this way to come up to Manchester. The four Liberty ships were viewed very much as stopgaps until new

One of the only Victory ships to come up to Manchester was Furness Pacific's *Pacific Stronghold* (1945), completed at the Bethlehem Fairfield Shipyard at Baltimore as the *Tusculum Victory*. On this trip she arrived home complete with a full deck cargo of timber. (John Clarkson)

purpose-built tonnage could be built, whereas the *Pacific Stronghold* was a longer-term investment. In this way, within two years of the end of the war Furness Pacific were back up to strength and back in business.

Two new purpose-built ships joined the fleet in 1948, the *Pacific Fortune* and *Pacific Unity*. The pair were not identical sisters, the *Pacific Fortune* being built at the Blythswood Shipbuilding Company in Scotstoun with a beam of 63 feet 5 inches whereas the *Pacific Unity* came from Laing's yard at Sunderland and she had a slightly wider beam of 63 feet 6 inches. This left a clearance in the locks of just 9 inches either side, the pair being the widest vessels then to have come up to Manchester. They were powered by steam turbines, the high pressure turbine connected through double reduction gears and the intermediate and low pressure turbines through single reduction gears to a single shaft to provide an impressive speed of 15½ knots. They had the normal two holds forward and two aft of the central superstructure, the holds served by an array of cargo handling gear. There was also First Class accommodation for twelve passengers.

The ships loaded cars and other luxury goods along with steel plate, metal fixings, machine parts and other specialist goods at Manchester. They left Manchester to call at Glasgow to load whisky in open stowage. If the dockies could not persuade the stowage officer to part with a bottle or two, they would bounce the next lift until they got what they wanted falling into their hands! The return journey included grain, pulp, newsprint and railway sleepers tied onto the deck. On a number of occasions, hurricanes in the Caribbean and rough weather in the North Atlantic saw the timber over the side as the lengths were too short to secure effectively. Fruit was also carried from the southern American ports and in all, the round trip was scheduled over three months with a departure every two weeks.

A major boost to the service was the arrangement that both Furness Pacific and the Harrison Line would share the Manchester berth for the West Indies. This pooling arrangement brought additional business to both companies as calls at the numerous ports involved, including Harrison's much-loved advertisement for '… and other islands as required', allowed more ships to call at fewer ports yet still carry broadly similar capacity loads. The bulk of the import trade was left in Harrison Line hands as the Pacific coast ships were already essentially fully loaded for home on entering the Panama Canal.

A major setback was the loss of the *Pacific Enterprise*, one of the original motor ships built for the service in 1927, on the Californian coast while on a voyage from Vancouver to Manchester loaded with grain. Merita Whatley explains in her book *Point Arena Lighthouse*:

Arena rock (Wash Rock) was one reason the US Lighthouse Bureau authorised building a lighthouse at Point Arena. The huge rock has a surface area of 1.24 acres. Submerged six feet under water at high tide and lying 1.5 miles offshore, it has a unique ecosystem and has snagged numerous ship's hulls over the centuries. Here on 9 September 1949 the 600 feet long *Pacific Enterprise*, a British freighter, went aground on Arena Rock. A thick fog shrouded the shoreline, the tower light was on, the fog signal horns called a warning of rocks nearby. The ship's Captain, M. E. Cogle, a 40 year veteran on his final voyage before retirement, believed he was just off the Farallon Islands, 20 miles south of Pont Reyes. All passengers and crew made it safely to shore. Some ships could be refloated on a high tide after grounding. The *Pacific Enterprise* was not so lucky; she broke into pieces on Arena Rock.

T. & J. Brocklebank also bought wartime standard ships as they had only ten ships afloat at the end of the war. In the war they had managed another ten ships for the Ministry of War Transport and three of the nine surviving ships were bought by the company. It had managed and crewed the *Empire Malacca*, built by Wiliam Gray at West Hartlepool in 1941, and in 1946 was able to purchase the ship and rename her *Mandasor*. The Canadian Fort-type ship *Fort Ville Marie* had been under Brocklebank management since she was commissioned in 1944, and she was bought in 1946 and given the name *Makalla* (see photo page 127). Finally, the company bought the Liberty ship *Samdee*, which it had managed since 1943, which in 1947 became the *Malabar*. They were obviously satisfied with the performance of the three ships as in 1956 they bought the one-time *Fort Enterprise*, which had enjoyed various owners since the war but now became the *Mahsud*. The following year the former *Stanford Victory* was chartered from the Prince Line (as the *British Prince*) for three years and traded under the name *Mandagala*.

In 1950, Brocklebank started a new triangular service outward via London to India, then to United States Gulf ports, returning to Liverpool and Manchester. This put Brocklebank ships on a regular schedule to Manchester rather than the part unloading of inbound ships as inducement dictated. A feature of the company's ships was tall funnels, and most of them had to have the tops of the funnels removed before they could come up the ship canal; they were in any case higher in the water for the return journey following unloading.

The Harrison Line had suffered severe losses during the war and they bought ten Liberty ships to replenish the fleet. The Liberty ships were the *Scholar*, ex-*Samidway* (see picture page 126); *Senator*, ex-*Sambay*; *Specialist*, ex-*Samwis*; *Student*, ex-*Samarinda*; and *Colonial*, formerly *Samovar* and for a brief period P. Henderson's *Kansi*; and *Historian*, formerly *Samaye* and briefly owned by Thomas Dunlop & Sons of Glasgow. A four ship purchase from Mollers, Hong Kong, provided the Liberty ships *Sculptor*, built as *Samcolne*; *Speaker* as *Sambalt*; *Statesman* as *Samgaudie*; and *Successor* as *Samhope*. Also, from the British government came four PF Standard ships built in British yards: the *Merchant*, formerly the *Empire Miranda*; *Naturalist*, previously *Empire Trumpet*; *Selector*, ex-*Empire Service*; and *Tribesman*, ex-*Empire Mandalay*. The company also ordered new ships and four more members of the pre-war *Settler* class were commissioned between 1947 and 1949.

The London-Greek tramp owners Counties Ship Management Company, whose ships ended with the suffix 'Hill', were often in the canal. They bought seven Liberty ships in 1947 and 1948 but sold them in order to help fund the purchase of thirty-four Canadian Fort- and Park-type ships (see picture of *Cedar Hill*, page 127). This was by

A spectacular picture of the *Pacific Exporter* (1928), having left Barton Lock and passing Harrison Line's *Sculptor* (1944), which is waiting off the small lock while the bigger ship passes by. The *Sculptor*, which was built as the Liberty ship *Samcolne*, can then enter the big lock, ready to proceed up to Manchester. (Manchester Ship Canal Company)

far the biggest collection of wartime standard ships in any one company flying the Red Ensign.

The Strick Line also bought one Liberty ship, which became familiar at Manchester. The *Samglory* was purchased in 1947 and renamed *Serbistan*. The company also started an earnest programme of building, receiving five new ships between the end of the war and the end of 1950. It was fortunate also in receiving licences to build a number of motor ships during the war.

While shipowners were able to buy the wartime surplus from government, they also set about ordering new ships. At first these were to pre-war designs; Harrison Line's *Settler* class, for example, had evolved through the 1930s and did so again in the late 1940s. Manchester Liners decided that new builds would be delivered in time to sustain the company business and did not buy any wartime surplus. The next ship of the *Manchester Port* Class was the *Manchester Regiment*. One final ship broadly of the same pre-war design, but with a more streamlined superstructure and broader funnel, was the *Manchester Merchant*, which was delivered in 1951. Both had oil-fired steam turbine engines.

The new boy on the block, as far as Manchester was concerned, was the Burberrys Steamship Company. Newsprint supplies were in short supply so the Burberrys

Strick Line's one and only Liberty ship, the *Serbistan* (1944), was a regular visitor to Manchester. She is seen from the air off Dover. (P&O)

No. 9 Dock with the Greek Liberty ship *Elene Stabatou* (1944) nearest on the north quay while opposite is the Liberty ship *Successor* (1944), ex-*Samhope*, owned by the Harrison Line, with one of that company's Settler-class steamers completed in the late 1930s and 1940s astern. Ahead of the *Successor* is a Brocklebank Line steamer with one of Manchester Liners' ships beyond. (Manchester Ship Canal Company)

The last of the pre-war design *Manchester Port* Class was ordered in 1949 and became the *Manchester Merchant* (1951). She is seen waiting at the Barton Lock Layby. (Author)

The *Caslon* (1949) was built for the Burberrys Steamship Company and transferred to Transatlantic Carriers in 1958. She is seen in Transatlantic Carriers colours outbound below Irwell Park Wharf in 1960. (Author)

company still had an important role to fulfil to enable the newspaper presses to turn out the daily papers. A new newsprint carrier, the *Baskerville*, was commissioned in 1946 as a replacement for the elderly *Pachesham*. The relatively modern *Kelmscott* was then replaced by another new ship, the *Caslon*. Progress with modernisation was marred in 1950 when the *Baskerville* was sold to the Bristol City Line, and a year later their elderly *London City*, which was then on charter from Turnbull Scott & Company of London, was acquired as the replacement and given the name *Chepman*.

The Prince Line had a fleet of seven ships dedicated to its Manchester and London services to the Mediterranean before the war. Two of the newer ships, the *Lancastrian Prince* and *Norman Prince*, were lost in the war, as also was the *Sardinian Prince* and *Cyprian Prince*. This left the company two ships short to resume the pre-war style Mediterranean services. Orders were placed with the Burntisland Shipbuilding Company in Fife, resulting in two very attractive-looking motor ships, the *Maltese Prince*, which was delivered in 1946, and the *Cyprian Prince*, which followed in 1949. Arrival of the *Maltese Prince* allowed the oldest ship in the fleet, the *Egyptian Prince*, which had been built in 1922, to be sold. The coal-burners *Palestinian Prince*, *Syrian Prince* and *Arabian Prince*, dating from 1936, were converted to oil-firing in 1946. The company now had a thoroughly modern fleet of Mediterranean traders, all of which had the corporate yacht-type appearance with comfortable accommodation and spacious public rooms for up to a dozen passengers.

The way that each shipowner dealt with rebuilding its fleet during the period of post-war shortages differed from company to company. Ellermans, for example, were able to buy twelve Liberty ships and set about a major programme of building mostly coal-fired turbine steamers, this method of propulsion being believed to be the most economical of the day.

Post-war, there was a significant increase in the number of destination ports regularly served from Manchester. This was a result of the increase in foreign flag companies now using Manchester as a terminal, not least near Continental services, with Swedish Lloyd, for example, regularly running to a variety of Swedish ports north-about Scotland, and Currie-Bugsier to German ports. On the long-haul routes, the acceptance of Scindia Steamship Company to the India Conference, which was formed during the war, was inevitable given the granting of independence to India and Pakistan in August 1947. The American demand to use its own ships is reflected in the increased use of Manchester by both the United States Lines Company and Lykes Line, the latter using Liberty ships as well as purpose-built ships.

In the early 1950s the one-time Manchester Spanish Line (Chapter 5), owned by H. Watson & Company, was still registered as a company and thoughts went to rejuvenating it. There was a strong Liverpool Conference to the Mediterranean, including MacAndrews, which was owned by Andrew Weir. As H. Watson & Company, former shipowners, now acted as agent for Andrew Weir in Manchester it seemed imprudent to enter into competition with them. The same applied to the Currie Line, working between London and Italian ports, so it was deemed unwise to proceed further with the idea. Watson did continue in business at Manchester and later set up a new shipping venture in 1981 (Chapter 12).

No. 9 Dock in about 1950 with the tramp steamer *Pencarrow* (1921), owned by the Chellew Navigation Company of Falmouth, on the left and the *American Scout* (1946), belonging to the United States Lines Company, on the right with two ships belonging to Manchester Liners beyond. The *American Scout* had a breadth of 63 feet, leaving little room for error in the locks, while much of her funnel has been left at Eastham. (Manchester Ship Canal Company)

Trade had almost fully recovered by the end of 1947. During the war years, the Port of Manchester had been exceptionally busy as east coast ports and London were not readily accessible due to enemy activity. This elevated importance is reflected in the port being the fourth most important in terms of the value of imports and exports in 1946, whereas it had only been the sixth most important in 1939. Even better, in 1947 and 1948 it became third most important, second only to London and Liverpool, before falling back to fourth place from 1949 onwards when Hull overtook Manchester.

It was increasingly common for Liverpool-based liner companies to send their ships up to Manchester to unload part cargoes. These could include bulk minerals from South America carried by the partner companies Royal Mail Line and Pacific Steam Navigation Company, or Palm Line ships up from Bromborough to unload hardwood from West Africa, perhaps also loading machinery and spares for the return voyage south. The ever-increasing procession of tramp ships was also involved in bulk cargoes, importing grain to No. 9 Dock, timber to Trafford Wharf and iron ore to Irlam.

Underpinning the importance of the Port of Manchester was its trade in oil and oil products. Farnie wrote:

Royal Mail Lines' *Pampas* (1944) discharging sulphur at the bulk goods facility at Irwell Park Wharf. (Author)

The Pacific Steam Navigation Company's *Salaverry* (1946) passing Barton Swing Aqueduct having part discharged at Manchester, on her way down to Liverpool to load for Pacific ports in South America. (Author)

The Ship Canal entered in 1946 upon an unprecedented period of ten consecutive years of increasing traffic as oil supplied 31per cent of the increment in export tonnage in 1948. The Middle East replaced the Caribbean as the leading exporter of oil in 1950, linking the traffic of the Ship Canal and the Suez Canal together as the largest flow of crude in history gathered momentum. The use of oil was vastly extended by its adoption in power stations and by the petrochemical revolution. Shell added a chemical plant at Stanlow in 1946-1949 so introducing a new industry to the UK, and then built an immense new oil refinery (1949-1951) at a cost of £15 million.

Typical sized tankers in the late 1940s were between 10,000 and 12,000 tons gross, all of which could be accommodated at Stanlow, and many could still berth at Barton and Mode Wheel. However, economy of scale indicated that tankers would have to become larger in size and plans to build ships of between 16,000 and 19,000 tons were announced by various owners in the late 1940s, with talk of 25,000-ton supertankers to follow.

By 1950 Shell had become the premier client of the ship canal company, and it was natural that it should look after that client. The ship canal company responded to the threat of larger and deeper tankers by seeking powers in 1949 to build a new oil terminal at Eastham, and it also set about raising the funds for its construction. The dock was to have its own separate entrance into the Mersey and was to be 40 feet deep. It was designed to accommodate four 'supertankers' of 25,000 tons, so allowing the port to retain its importance in the oil trade. However, it would take four and a half years before this new facility was ready for business.

The BP Tanker Company's *British Councillor* (1948) was typical of the tankers seen in the canal, here at Latchford, that were part of the post-war fleet rebuilding programme. (Author)

On the domestic routes, Coast Lines did not reopen the regular liner service to London. It did, however, maintain the twice-weekly service to Glasgow inherited all those years ago from M. Langlands & Sons. There was also the weekly sailing to Dublin by British & Irish and the twice-weekly departure for Belfast. The Belfast, Mersey & Manchester Steamship Company ceased calling at Manchester in 1947, serving only Liverpool and Bromborough.

The Belfast Steamship Company now assumed sole responsibility for the Manchester trade and commenced a twice-weekly service between that port and Belfast. Two elderly ships in the Coast Lines fleet were brought onto the service and renamed the *Ulster Merchant* and *Ulster Mariner*. They sailed twice a week while the *Ulster Coast* occasionally deputised. The service was advertised under the banner Belfast Steamship Company and Belfast, Mersey & Manchester Steamship Company, although the ships of the latter company rarely came up to Manchester.

The near Continental routes were busy, not least to supply the British military now stationed in Germany. Regular liner services to Scandinavia, the Baltic countries, Germany and Denmark, Holland, Belgium and France now existed with both British and foreign companies involved. These included British & Continental, Muller Line and Ellerman's Wilson under the Red Ensign, the Danish United Steamship Company, Finland Steamship Company, Currie-Bugsier, Hollandsche Stoomboot Maatschappij N V, the Norwegian Thor Thoresen Line, and Swedish Lloyd.

British & Continental operated an increasingly diverse network of services serving France, Belgium and Holland, from Glasgow, Liverpool, Manchester and Belfast. The frequency of services from Manchester was weekly to Amsterdam and Rotterdam, weekly to Antwerp and Ghent and fortnightly to Dunkirk. The company lost nearly all its younger fleet members in the war, and three new ships were commissioned in 1946: the *Lestris*, *Kittiwake* and *Merganser*, sister ships of about 2,000 tons gross. The *Merganser*, however, was lost the following year in a collision in the River Scheldt; making the final turn in the river into the docks at Antwerp, the *Merganser* was run down by the American steamer *Norwalk Victory*. It was later revealed that the American ship had a steering defect and her rudder was not responding to the helm. She was wholly blamed for the accident for not anchoring on becoming aware of the fault.

The *Merganser* was replaced by a second-hand purchase from the Dundee, Perth & London Shipping Company, the *Dundee*, which was given the name *Dotterel*. She was converted from coal- to oil-firing and operated on only two of her three boilers, her normal speed of 12½ knots being too fast to accomplish the voyage on the normal two days and a night schedule in time to work cargo the next morning as she would have arrived in the middle of the night. Two rather fine oil-burning ships were delivered by Cammell Laird in 1949. These were the *Ardetta* and *Bittern*, very similar to the earlier *Kittiwake* Class, although smaller at just 1,500 tons gross. This pair brought the fleet back up to the pre-war strength of twelve ships. A third ship, almost identical to the *Ardetta* and *Bittern*, the *Clangula*, was delivered by Cammell Laird in 1954.

There were a couple of minor accidents in the canal. On 18 July 1948, the small tanker *Helmsley II* struck and breached the lower lock gates in the small lock at Eastham. The

The British & Continental Steamship Company's *Clangula* (1954) heading down the canal adjacent to the Barton Oil Wharf. (Author)

The old paddle tugs were disposed of after the war; here the crew of the paddle tug *Eccles* (1905) pose for the camera.

Fog was always a problem on the ship canal; the *Eccles* (1905) noses her way along in company with a screw tug, ready for the next tow.

ship fell by 8 feet as water gushed out into the Mersey. Fortunately the upper gate shut and saved the water in the canal from discharging into the river. In November 1952, a similar accident occurred when the Swedish Lloyd steamer *Caledonia* hit the lock gates, causing a breach closing the canal for two days. On 16 July 1950, the outbound West Hartlepool Steam Navigation Company's tramp steamer *Hendonhall* (7,359 tons gross) collided with William Robertson's coaster *Citrine* coming up the canal. The accident happened 7 miles above Eastham. Both ships were damaged, the *Citrine* coming off worst.

The canal tugs were progressively updated after the war and the old paddle tugs were withdrawn one by one. Most had gone by 1951; the *Irlam* and *Eccles* were the last to go.

Chapter 10

The Fabulous Fifties

The breadth of services offered from Manchester in the 1950s was immense. In 1952 H. Watson were agents for the Lykes Line's regular service to and from New Orleans, Houston and Galveston; the fortnightly Currie-Bugsier joint service to Hamburg and Bremen; Hellenic Line's service to various Greek ports; the regular Coker Line service to Abo, Helsingfors, Kotka and several Swedish ports; Muller Line's direct sailings to Paris and also to Rouen, with departures from Manchester every few days; the Knutsen Line service to the Pacific; and Lauritzen Line's service to west coast Italian ports and Sicily. The Coker Line also operated a joint service with the Finland Steamship Company to Norrköping, Stockholm, Gefle and Sundsvall, while Swedish Lloyd offered a regular service from Manchester to Gothenburg, Malmö, Helsingborg and Holmstad. Other regular services included Manchester Liners, Furness Pacific and the United States Lines running to Canada and the United States; Clan Lines to South and East African ports; Strick Line to the Persian Gulf; and Prince Line to Tunis, Malta, Tripoli in Libya, Benghazi, Tobruk, Alexandria, Beirut, Tripoli in Syria, Lattakia, Iskenderun, Mersin, Limassol, Larnaca, Famagusta, Tel Aviv and Haifa.

A new service was commenced in 1952 by Manchester Liners. There were plans for a ship canal to be constructed that would allow large seagoing ships into the Great Lakes. Manchester Liners was keen to show their flag to potential customers in the Lakes region, so that when the day came they would already have a customer base. The idea was to join the various European companies that had been running small, specially built steamers – snub-nosed 'Lakers' – up to Toronto via the Welland Canal since before the Second World War in order to develop trade directly to Manchester. Two rather special little ships were ordered from Cammell Laird at Birkenhead; their outline design was based on that developed for the *Ardetta* and *Bittern*, delivered to the British & Continental Steamship Company in 1949 (see Chapter 9). The main difference was that the two Lakers would be equipped with an oil-fired steam turbine engine, making them some of the smallest ever turbine-driven ships.

The new ships were launched as *Manchester Pioneer* and *Manchester Explorer* and were ready in time for the 1952 summer ice-free season, sailing to Toronto and

UNITED STATES LINES

AMERICA FRANCE LINE   ORIOLE LINE
AMERICAN HAMPTON ROADS/YANKEE LINE

FAST PASSENGER & FREIGHT SERVICES

NEW YORK

BOSTON, PHILADELPHIA, BALTIMORE & HAMPTON ROADS

From LONDON   *Receiving
(b)SOUTHSTAR ... ... Aug 23—28
(c)(a)AMERICAN FLYER ... Aug 30—Sept 4
Loading Berth: "D" Shed, Victoria Dock.
*New York and/or Boston only, closing 24 hours earlier
for other ports.

From LIVERPOOL   Receiving
(d)AMERICAN VETERAN ... ... Aug 19—28
(d)AMERICAN PACKER ... ... Sept 2—11
Loading Berth: N.E. No. 2, Gladstone Dock.

From MANCHESTER   Receiving
(g)(d)AMERICAN PACKER Aug 28—Sept 7(noon)
(g)(d)AMERICAN CHIEF Sept 11—21 (noon)
Loading Berth: No. 2 Shed, No. 9 Dock, Salford.

From GLASGOW   *Receiving
(e)AMERICAN SCIENTIST Aug 29—Sept 4
(e)AMERICAN PRESS ... Sept 12—18
Loading Berth: 6, Yorkhill Basin.
*New York and/or Boston only, closing 24 hours
earlier for other ports.

EXPRESS SERVICE from SOUTHAMPTON
         clos.   sail
‡UNITED STATES ... ... Aug 28   Aug 29
World's Fastest Liner.
*AMERICA ... ... Sept 9   Sept 10
Popular Transatlantic Luxury Ship.
‡Cargo bookings subject to special agreement
Berths: ‡10/3. *10/.

From HULL   Receiving
STEAMER ... ... To be announced

From DUBLIN   Receiving
(f)(e)AMERICAN SCIENTIST ... Aug 27—28
(f)(e)AMERICAN PRESS ... ... Sept 10—11
Loading Berth: North Wall Extension.

(a)New York, Philadelphia, Baltimore, Hampton
Roads. (b) New York. Boston, Philadelphia,
Baltimore. (c) Via Havre. (d) New York,
Boston, Philadelphia, Baltimore, Hampton
Roads. (e) Boston, New York, Philadelphia,
Baltimore, Hampton Roads. (f) Via Glasgow.
(g) Via Liverpool.

Also from BRISTOL CHANNEL PORTS

CONTINENTAL SAILINGS

For New York & East Coast Out Ports—
Weekly from Hamburg . Bremen . Rotterdam
Antwerp . Le Havre . Every 4 weeks from
Bordeaux and Bilbao

VESSELS LOADING FOR HAMPTON ROADS WILL
ACCEPT CARGO FOR NORFOLK AND NEWPORT NEWS

SOUTH ATLANTIC LINE

Freight Services Only

CHARLESTON, SAVANNAH, JACKSONVILLE
& other ports in the range as inducement offers

From LONDON   Receiving
*SOUTHWIND ... ... Late Sept
†SOUTHLAND ... ... Mid Sept

From DUBLIN   Receiving
†THOS. NELSON ... ... Ear Sept

From LIVERPOOL   Receiving
†THOS. NELSON ... ... Ear Sept

From GLASGOW   Receiving
†THOS. NELSON ... ... Ear Sept

From MANCHESTER   Receiving
†THOS NELSON ... ... Ear Sept
†Also calling Wilmington. *Also calls Miami

Executive and Head Passenger Office :
50, PALL MALL, LONDON, S.W.1 *WHItehall 5454*
Head Freight Office: **38, LEADENHALL STREET,
LONDON E.C.3** *ROYal 6677*

United States Lines and South Atlantic Line
advertisement, Monday 19 August 1957. (*Lloyd's
List and Shipping Gazette*)

The *Manchester Pioneer* (1952) above Barton, outbound for the St Lawrence Seaway and Great Lakes ports after she had been extended in 1960. (Author)

other ports as inducement demanded. The Welland Canal allowed only 3 inches spare width to the ships in some locks and could accommodate a draught of just 14 feet. The service was soon extended to Chicago. The first year of service into the Lakes was a success and late in 1952 the six-year-old Norwegian Laker *Vigør* was bought, refitted and given the name *Manchester Prospector*. Two more small Lakers were commissioned in 1956: the first motor ships in the fleet, the *Manchester Vanguard* and *Manchester Venture*. These had the engines and cramped accommodation aft, but were hugely successful in developing trade for the company in the Lakes. When ice closed the season in the autumn the Lakers were chartered for the Mediterranean fruit season, Yeoward Brothers generally taking the two new motor ships on charter for the winter.

A few minutes before the *Manchester Pioneer* was launched at Cammell Laird's yard at Birkenhead, the oil-burning turbine steamer *Manchester Spinner* also took to the water. She was designed for the conventional Canadian service but was important as she was the first ship in the fleet to include modern post-war developments and the first to break the mould of the *Manchester Port* Class, dating from the mid-1930s. The *Manchester Spinner* was an attractive-looking ship with accommodation and engines in the conventional amidships position. She was fast, with a design speed of 15 knots. A sister ship, the *Manchester Mariner*, was delivered in 1955. An even faster ship came from Harland & Wolff at Belfast in 1959, the ugly duckling *Manchester Miller*, and fit for an impressive 17 knots against a heavy oil

The *Manchester Mariner* (1955), heading down the canal above Barton Locks, was the last traditional engines-and-superstructure-amidships-type vessel to be built for Manchester Liners. (Author)

fuel bill for her boilers. She is described in *Manchester Liners – An Extraordinary Story*:

> The *Manchester Miller* was flush decked and had an amidships bridge structure with two hatches forward and three aft. She required a crew of 50 officers and men. Like her predecessors she had twelve passenger berths in single and twin berth cabins, a saloon and small smoke room. The ship offered a massive 600,000 cubic feet hold space and was designed to the optimum dimensions of the Ship Canal at Manchester. The bridge front of the vessel had a modernistic curve to it that was really the only discerning outward feature of the whole vessel, as placed right aft were twin uptakes abreast each disguised as Samson posts, which provided a distinctly unbalanced and spiky profile.

The St Lawrence Seaway opened in 1959 and the Lakers were superseded by middle-sized ships specially built to develop the bulk trades from the Great Lakes. These were the motor ships *Manchester Fame* and *Manchester Faith*. Their role was to develop the trade, supported still by the five small Lakers. The sailing schedules included Detroit, Chicago, Cleveland and Duluth with an option to load at Montreal on return if space allowed. Space did not allow for long and the new twins were soon fully loaded in the Great Lakes ports with grain for Manchester and lard in special deep tanks. In 1960, the large turbine steamer *Manchester Progress* ran up to Duluth to load a full cargo of grain and edible oils. The new service put such a strain on the fleet that ships had to be chartered in: *Western Prince* and *Southern Prince* came from the Prince Line round-the-world service and ships from Irish Shipping, such as the *Irish Alder*, *Irish Larch* and *Irish Elm,* also flew the Manchester Liners house flag.

Four more steam turbine ships were built for the Furness Withy Pacific coast service in the 1950s: the *Pacific Reliance* in 1951, *Pacific Northwest* in 1954, and the *Pacific Envoy* and *Pacific Stronghold* in 1958. They were all essentially similar and based on the design of the *Pacific Fortune* and *Pacific Unity*, completed in 1948. All six ships had a respectable service speed of 15½ knots, offered up to 140,000 cubic feet of refrigerated space and comfortable accommodation for twelve passengers. The arrival of the *Pacific Reliance* in service allowed the Victory ships *Pacific Ranger* and *Pacific Importer* to be sold and the *Pacific Liberty* and *Pacific Nomad* were disposed of once the *Pacific Northwest* was in service. The Victory ship *Pacific Stronghold* was retained until 1959.

Somebody somewhere clearly had a sense of duty coupled with a sense of fun. The first letter of the second name of each ship commissioned between the *Pacific Furness* and the *Pacific Stronghold* spelled the word 'Furnes'; sadly the ship named with the second 'S' was never commissioned and the word 'Furness' remained incomplete.

The Prince Line also continued to commission new motor ships for its Mediterranean services from Manchester and London. The *Egyptian Prince* was commissioned in 1951, and the *Black Prince* in 1954. The next pair, the *Norman Prince* and *Northumbrian Prince*, was slightly smaller. The *Scottish Prince* joined the fleet in 1957, having been commissioned for associate company Shaw, Savill & Albion Company as the *Afric* in 1950. The last ship of this handsome class of small Prince Line vessels was the larger *Lancastrian Prince*. All were regular visitors to Manchester and all offered excellent accommodation for twelve passengers. However, a downturn in the Mediterranean trades at the end of the 1950s caused the order for a sister ship to the *Lancastrian Prince* to be cancelled.

T. & J. Brocklebank's new triangular service from India to the Gulf ports, loading at Manchester, Liverpool and London, meant that its ships came up the canal every two weeks. Most had tall funnels that needed attention at the crane wharf at Eastham before they could proceed on to Manchester.

Paper and pulp continued to be a large import commodity into the ship canal. The Burberrys Steamship Company continued to load newsprint in Canada for discharge in Manchester or London. Newsprint was occasionally also brought in from the Baltic. New ships were the *Isaac Carter*, delivered in 1952 and equipped with obsolescent triple expansion engines, and the *Baskerville*, which followed two years later and had a more efficient combination triple steam expansion engine and low pressure turbine. The first purpose-built motor ship was the *Caxton*, delivered in 1958; the old *Caxton* and the *Chepman* were both sold in 1957. Now that newsprint was freely available to the newspapers again in the UK, the work of the Burberrys Steamship Company was done. The company, with its four ships, including the steamer *Caslon* dating from 1949, was sold late in 1958 to a consortium of five Canadian paper manufacturing companies to become the London-based shipping company Transatlantic Carriers. The

Sunday afternoon trip to Latchford Lock: Prince Line's *Western Prince* (1955), on charter to Manchester Liners, bound for Montreal on 31 March 1963. (Author)

The *Pacific Reliance* (1951), topmasts lowered, approaching Eastham Lock in the custody of two of the three Furness Withy tugs based at Liverpool.

The *Norman Prince* (1956) was one of the many yacht-like Prince Line motor ships built after the war. She is seen heading down the canal below the Barton Bridges. (Author)

names of the ships remained unchanged and they continued to visit Manchester to unload newsprint on a regular basis.

Bowater opened its paper mill at Ellesmere Port in 1931 and constructed a wharf alongside the ship canal to import timber and pulp. Bowater relied heavily on chartering after the war. As costs increased due to demand, particularly at the height of the Korean War, the company decided to expand its own ship-owning interests. Three magnificent big newsprint carriers, each powered by a steam turbine engine, were delivered from Denny's yard at Dumbarton: the sisters *Sarah Bowater* and *Margaret Bowater* in 1955, and the flagship *Nicolas Bowater* in 1958. In the holds, the usual structural pillars were kept to a minimum and spars were coated in soft rubber in order to protect the newsprint rolls. There were no 'tween decks as the newsprint rolls were stacked vertically end to end from the floor of the hold to the main deck, each line of rolls separated by flat dunnage to protect them. In 1957, the management of the fleet passed to Cayzer Irvine (Clan Line), and crewing became fully integrated with Clan Line and its associates.

Another newsprint carrier joined the fleet in 1959, the *Markland*, also a Denny product built in 1953 for the Mersey Paper Company of Liverpool, Nova Scotia, which was taken over by Bowater. Two smaller ships, the *Liverpool Rover* and *Liverpool Packet*, also came under Bowater Steamship Company ownership through the same deal. The success of shipowning over the risks involved in chartering led also to six smaller 4,000 gross ton motor ships being commissioned as pulp carriers, importing from Canada and Scandinavia. They were also used to carry newsprint to the eastern seaboard and into the Great Lakes. This was the *Elizabeth Bowater* Class, built between 1958 and 1961, all of which were regular visitors to Ellesmere Port.

The *Sarah Bowater* (1955), one of three steam turbine-driven newsprint carriers built for the Bowater Steamship Company.

Bowater's newsprint carrier *Liverpool Rover* (1929).

But it was the oil trade that really took off in the 1950s. Tankers were slowly increasing in size and it was realised that Stanlow would soon no longer be able to accommodate the larger tankers then being built or planned. Westminster Dredging Company was awarded the contract to deepen the Eastham Channel in anticipation of the deep draught tankers expected at the new dock at Eastham. The entrance lock was directly off the Mersey and was 100 feet wide with a depth of 40 feet. The Queen Elizabeth II Dock received its first ship on 19 January 1954 when the Shell tanker *Velletia* arrived from Kuwait. She delivered a full cargo of 28,000 tons of crude oil. The *Velletia* was a typical large tanker of the day, of 18,661 tons gross, completed in 1952.

Oil supplies had been seriously interrupted when the government of Iran nationalised the assets of the Anglo-American Oil Company in March 1951 – the Abadan Crisis. Kuwait was developed as a substitute for Iran, but larger ships were needed for this trade, hence the new supertankers. When the Suez Canal was closed in 1956, even larger tankers were needed for the run round the Cape, and at this point Shell was forced to abandon Eastham in favour of the newly built Tranmere Oil Terminal, just above Birkenhead. Tranmere eventually opened for business on 8 June 1960 when Shell's 38,000-ton deadweight tanker *Zenatia* came alongside. The terminal was owned by the Mersey Docks & Harbour Board and the transfer of the larger tankers to Tranmere had a severe impact on Manchester's import statistics, even though the oil was sent overland by pipeline to Stanlow some 15 miles away. The year 1959 thus became the peak year for trade to the port of Manchester.

Tankers still used both Stanlow and the Queen Elizabeth II Dock but no longer in the numbers previously enjoyed. The days when tankers queued up to berth at Stanlow had ended. Barton still had regular tanker traffic, mainly dealing in import of partly refined products and exporting smaller parcels of specialist oil products such as lubricants.

The Abadan Crisis had a direct impact on the Persian Gulf service maintained by the Strick Line. Departures from Manchester were cut back from twice a month to monthly until replacement export loads could be built up. Recovery was nevertheless rapid as the burgeoning oil industry in Kuwait soon demanded plant and machinery to be shipped out from manufacturers in the Manchester region.

The Strick Line lost an almost brand-new ship in tragic circumstances. Before she ever had a chance to come up to Manchester, the *Seistan*, delivered only in July 1957 and a sister to the *Karaghistan*, reported a fire on 17 February 1958 in No. 5 hold beneath the explosives magazine. She was bound for Khorramshahr with general cargo from London, which included 170 tons of explosives, fuses and detonators. On 18 February she anchored 2 miles east of South Sitra Beacon, Bahrain, and some 75 tons of explosives were discharged into a barge. Some of the explosives had partly liquefied, indicating that the explosives had become unstable.

Before the rest of the explosives could be taken off, the fire spread to the magazine, causing a massive explosion just after 9 p.m. It destroyed the after part of the vessel and much of the superstructure. Sadly, fifty-three members of the crew, including the master, and five men in the tug *Suhail* alongside, died in the blast. The *Suhail*

The tanker *Caltex Kenya* was a regular visitor to the Barton Oil Wharf in the early 1960s. After discharging she had to go up through Mode Wheel Lock to turn before she could come back down the canal. (Author)

Strick Line's *Karaghistan* (1957) inbound above the Barton Bridges with a large part of her funnel on the deck ready for painting while in Manchester. (Author)

completely disintegrated and disappeared. It was believed but never proven that a small consignment of toe puffs, chemically impregnated cotton hardened for the toe part of a shoe, had spontaneously ignited.

During the 1950s the so-called cheap flags-of-convenience ships registered in Liberia and Panama were making inroads on conventional liner trades by undercutting Conference rates. 'Flagging-out' minimises tax payments and avoids the application of health, safety and environmental standards of the home countries. The practice started in the 1920s when American shipowners, frustrated with the increasing burden and cost of incoming American maritime regulations, reflagged their ships to Panama. The similar open registry in Liberia started in 1948 following the sale of numerous cheap wartime surplus vessels by America after the Second World War. Manchester started to see both Panama City and Liberia as ports of registry on ships trading to a variety of regions otherwise controlled by the Conferences. Tankers and bulk carriers were increasingly flagged-out.

The Hollandsche Stoomboot Maatschappij received a 'new' motor ship for its Manchester and Liverpool service to Amsterdam. She was the *Texelstroom*, built in 1947 for C. Clausen of Copenhagen with the name *Dorrit Clausen*, time chartered to Yeoward brothers of Liverpool until she was sold to Hollandsche Stoomboot in 1949. She was of similar deadweight to her former namesake (see Chapter 7) that maintained the service before the war and was sunk by torpedo in February 1941. Both ships offered berths for twelve passengers, with the round trip sold during the summer months as a popular ten-day cruise holiday with shore excursions laid on while the ship was at Amsterdam.

The British & Continental Steamship Company was back up to its pre-war strength following a rebuilding programme in the late 1940s and early 1950s. However, by 1954 trading conditions from west coast ports to the Low Countries had become difficult and six ships were sold in the space of two years. These included the nine-year-old steamers *Kittiwake* and *Lestris*. Then, in 1957 the *Ousel*, which had been built for the Cork Steamship Company in 1922, was lost in a collision in the Mersey on her way up to Manchester, as Colin Turner describes in *Sea Breezes* from December 1982:

> The scene of her loss was between Tranmere and New Ferry in the River Mersey, where she was anchored on the morning of 8 January awaiting entry into the Manchester Ship Canal. At around 2 am she was run into by the Panamanian tanker *Liverpool* which had been pursuing a down-river course, having left the Queen Elizabeth II Oil Dock at Eastham a little while earlier. The *Ousel* was holed and, with a cargo consisting mainly of steel ingots and girders, began to settle rapidly. No less than five tugs came to her assistance and they were successful in beaching her. However, after the tugs had been dismissed, the *Ousel* slid down the bank on the ebbing tide and settled in deeper water.

The *Ousel* incident did not deter the British & Continental company from selling yet another ship, the *Egret*, later in the year. The company recognised that its triple steam expansion engine ships were no longer economical running in competition with small

Dutch motor ships with a crew of just a few men. It rose to this challenge by ordering its first and only motor vessel, a new *Egret*, delivered in 1959, and made up for the shortfall in vessels by chartering as required. By 1960 the company flag was rarely seen in the canal although infrequent services were still advertised to Dunkirk and to Amsterdam and Rotterdam.

The Irish Sea services were also near their end, as Robert Sinclair describes in his history of the Belfast Steamship Company:

> ... in November 1954, the *Jersey Coast* and *Guernsey Coast* returned from the Channel Islands to become the *Ulster Weaver* and *Ulster Spinner*. They enabled the coal-burning *Ulster Merchant* and *Ulster Mariner* to be disposed of for breaking up. Their British Polar diesels brought modern tonnage at last to the Manchester trade which they served until it was discontinued at the end of 1963. Interestingly their single screws were driven in opposite directions from each other and it is thought that their engines were originally intended for one twin screw vessel.

The *Denbigh Coast* was on relief duties on the Manchester service when she sailed for Belfast on 18 July 1960. She met with an untimely end before she had even left the Mersey when she collided with the big freighter *Irish Maple*. The *Denbigh Coast* sank within ten minutes. No lives were lost.

The motor ship *Ulster Weaver* (1936) maintained the twice-weekly Manchester–Belfast service from November 1954 onwards jointly with the *Ulster Spinner* (1942). The *Ulster Weaver* is outbound above the Barton Oil Wharf. (Author)

The British & Irish service to Dublin survived a little longer than the Belfast service, although disaster struck almost on the last sailing, as described in the history of the Tyne-Tees Steam Shipping Company:

> The main employment of the *Wicklow* was on the cargo service between Liverpool and Dublin, but she also operated to Cork, Dundalk and Drogheda and from Manchester from time to time. Indeed it was a trip to Manchester in late September 1964, when her engineers could not put her almost brand new machinery in reverse, and she collided with lock gates so closing the Manchester Ship Canal to navigation for the next three days. The *Wicklow* was undamaged and two weeks after her 'three days of fame' she took the very last sailing from Manchester to Dublin for the British & Irish company.

The claim of widest ship to navigate to Manchester changed hands in autumn 1954 when the brand new *Swiftpool*, belonging to Sir R. Ropner & Company (Pool Shipping Company) came up to Manchester with a cargo of grain. She had a beam of 63 feet 7 inches, leaving just 8½ inches of clearance either side at the inland locks. She was just one of a never-ending procession of tramp ships chartered for a variety of trades the world over. The ships increasingly flew foreign flags, but British ships were still in the majority for much of the 1950s. They varied in size from some of the smaller vessels owned by Stephens Sutton to the larger ships belonging to Ropner and other tramp ship operators. There were also the Russian timber ships, which went up the canal to discharge at Trafford Wharf. Most of these were elderly steamers dating from the 1920s and earlier, but they were an impressive sight on the canal with their deck cargo loaded almost to the bridge windows.

The iron and steel works at Irlam and Warrington were nationalised in 1951 as part of the British Iron & Steel Corporation. That organisation along with Houlder Brothers of London together formulated a concept for purpose-built iron ore carriers of about 9,000 tons deadweight that could serve the small harbour at Port Talbot and, of course, be able to navigate the Manchester Ship Canal. Until then conventional single-deck tramp ships had been used for the trade. A new jointly owned shipping company was registered as Ore Carriers in 1954 to manage the first pair of ships, the *Orelia* and *Oreosa*. The ships were innovative in that they had no 'tween decks, but had clear decks with very large and wide hatches to facilitate fast unloading with grab cranes, and the engines, bridge and accommodation were right aft. Four further ships were commissioned over the next two years: *Oredian*, *Oregis*, *Orepton* and *Oremina*. They all came up to Irlam Wharf to discharge and then continued up to Manchester to turn before descending the canal to go to sea again.

Similar ore carriers were built for other companies in the charter business, and these ships were also regular visitors to Irlam. Six were ordered by J. & J. Denholm and jointly owned by the British Iron & Steel Corporation, and others were owned by Denholm subsidiary companies and the Bamburgh Shipping Company (owned by W. A. Souter & Company of Newcastle). The ships were highly profitable both to the shipping company and to the British Iron & Steel Corporation, which enjoyed cheap freight rates, as David Burrell explains in his book on Furness Withy:

MANCHESTER—IN PORT

Vessel	Tons Gross Dk. or Bth. Broker
AEGIR, 299, Ellesmere Port, F. Armitt	
ALICIA, 5026, Eastham, H. Watson & Co.	
ALIGNITY, 893, Stuart's Wf., Stanlow, F. Armitt	
AMERICAN VETERAN, 8279, Shed 2. Dk. 9, Benju. Ackerley & Son	
ARDETTA, 1542. Shed 8. Dk. 8. J. T. Fletcher	
AWARDITY, 479, Weaste, Bromport Transport	
BARON GLENCONNER, 5468, Irwell Park Wf., Thor. Thoresen	
CALYX, 212, Slate Wf., A. E. Bowen	
CAXTON, 7271, Shed 1, Trafford Wf., H. Watson	
CLARITY, 750, Ellesmere Port, F. Armitt	
DABAIBE, 3741, Ellesmere Port, H. Tyrer & Co.	
ESSO TIOGA, 797, Eastham, H. Watson	
FYRUN, 498, Partington, Vogt & Maguire	
GOOTE, 490, Shed 4, Dk. 6, Wilson, Son & Co.	
HAZELFIELD, 692, Partington, A. E. Bowen	
HEMSLEY I, 1178, Stanlow Lay Bye, Houlder Bros. & Co.	
HINDSHOLM, 1522, Shed 7, Dk. 8. A. Knudsen	
HOLMFIELD, 560, Sun Mills, A. E. Bowen	
IDUNA, 400, Sheds 2 & 4, Dk. 6, H. Watson	
ILA, 1344, Shed 9. Dk. 9. Thor. Thoresen	
IMMEN, 1500, Ellesmere Port, Ell. Wilson	
IREX, 8280, Weaste, Thor. Thoresen	
IRISH HOLLY, 2940, Stanlow 3, E. H. Mundy	
KHASIELLA, 12,119, Stanlow 4, Brinings	
LAIRDSBROOK, 761, Shed 4. Dk. 4, Coast Lines	
LANCASHIRE COAST, 1283, Ellesmere Port, Coast Lines	
LEVENSAU, 1310, Eastham, H. Watson	
LOCH MADDY, 7088, Irlam Ore Wf., H. Watson & Co.	
MANCHESTER CITY, 7296, Eastham, Manchester Liners	
MANCHESTER EXPLORER, 1805, Eastham, Manchester Liners	
MANCHESTER MERCHANT, 7651, Shed 10. Dk. 9. Manchester Liners	
MANCHESTER PIONEER, 1805, Shed 6. Dk. 9. Manchester Liners	
MANCHESTER PROGRESS, 7346, Shed 8, Dk. 9. Manchester Liners	
MARIA LUISA, 2802, Shed 1, Dk. 9. Sivewright, Bacon & Co.	
MENAPIA, 1000, Partington, A. E. Bowen	
MUPHRID-N., 494, Ellesmere Port, H. Tyrer	
NESSAND, 654, Ince, E. H. Mundy & Co.	
NORMAN PRINCE, 2709, Shed 6. Dk. 7, Gough & Crosthwaite	
OTTERBERG, 1754, Ellesmere Port, Sivewright Bacon & Co.	
PANAMOLGA, Irwell Park Wf., H. Watson	
PASS OF KINTAIL, 913, Stuart's Wf., Stanlow, H. Watson & Co.	
PORT TALBOT, 250, Runcorn, F. Armitt	
POSEIDON, 1400, Ellesmere Port, Sivewright, Bacon & Co.	
PUNTARENAS, 4928, Eastham, H. Watson	
ROYBANK, 7368, Shed 7, Dk. 9. H. Watson	
SHELL DIRECTOR, 891, Ellesmere Port, E. H. Mundy & Co.	
SHELL DRILLER, 969, Stuart's Wf., Stanlow, E. H. Mundy & Co.	
SHELL SUPPLIER, 1167, Stanlow 1, E. H Mundy & Co.	
SIGNE, 1406, Partington, Vogt & Maguire	
SILVIA, 490, Shed 4, Dk. 8. Bahr, Behrend	
STAD ARNHEM, 5215, Irwell Park Lay-Bye, H Watson & Co.	
SYDHAV, 10,946, Berth 4, Queen Elizabeth II Dk., Brinings	
THAMES, 400, Shed 3, Trafford Wf., A. E. Bowen	
THE LADY GWENDOLEN, 1165, Shed 1A. Riverside Qv., A. Guinness, Son & Co.	
TRANSCASTOR, 9097, Berth 1, Q. Elizabeth II Dk., Toft & Co.	
WIMBORNE, 368, Weston Point, I.C.I.	
ZOELLA LYKES, 6829, Shed 4, Dk. 9. H. Watson & Co.	

Ships in Port, Thursday 22 August 1957. (*Lloyd's List and Shipping Gazette*)

The *Ripley* (1953), owned by Stephens Sutton, was one of many tramp ships coming up to Manchester in the 1950s and early 1960s. (Author)

The innovative ore carrier *Oreosa* (1954), her hatches open after discharging iron ore at Irlam, then went up to Manchester to turn before she returned down the canal, where she is seen above the Barton Oil Wharf before loading coal at Partington. (Author)

One of the bulk ore carriers developed from the *Oreosa* type vessel was Buries Markes' *La Colina* (1958), seen beneath the M62 bridge approaching Barton Locks, having discharged her cargo at Lancashire Steel Company's Irlam Wharf. (Author)

The Dutch style glass-topped launch *MSC Silver Arrow* (1953). She was used for promotional purposes and educational cruises round the docks and down to the Barton Bridges and back. The *MSC Silver Arrow* was succeeded by a similar but larger launch, the *Silver Arrow II*, in 1969. (Manchester Ship Canal Company)

The trade for which the ore carriers were built was one way only. Rather than return to the loading ports in ballast, it was policy for the ships to take coal charters out. Coal exports at the time exceeded iron ore imports so it proved possible to finance the ships from outward earnings and treat the ore cargo homewards as a ballast run at cheaper freight rates. The design proved to be a handy and efficient one; the ship's quick discharge invariably earned bonus payments from charterers and they were always in demand.

The bulk ore carrier concept was also developed into many themes by British and overseas owners. One of the British shipowners that built several ore carriers to a variety of designs was Buries Markes of London, whose vessel *La Colina* was regularly on the berth at Irlam.

In 1955, the cable-laying ship *Ocean Layer* came up the Manchester Ship Canal to load cable from the Trafford Park Works of W. T. Glover & Company, destined for British Columbia. The cable was 93½ miles long and was designed to connect Vancouver Island with the mainland.

The canal company had a small launch used to show visitors around the dock system and the upper part of the canal. The Dutch river bus *MSC Silver Arrow* was built in Holland in 1953 and bought by the public relations department of the Manchester Ship Canal Company in 1957. Based at No. 6 Dock, she was used to show guests of the company around the dock system, locking down at Mode Wheel to pass under the Barton Bridges on the deep water side, turn and come up past the Bridges in the narrow channel on the Eccles side of the canal. The round trip lasted nearly two hours. Apart from these short promotional cruises, she was also used for educational trips with parties of schoolchildren. The *MSC Silver Arrow* was succeeded in 1969 by a similar, but larger and specially built launch, the *MSC Silver Arrow II*. This new launch could accommodate fifty-eight seated passengers.

Chapter 11

Accidents, Tragedy and Strikes

The 1960s started with major incidents involving regular canal traffic and ended with the Bob's Ferry disaster. On 21 March 1961, at about 5.45 p.m., the sand hopper *Mary P Cooper*, carrying sand dredged from the Mersey Estuary, collided head-on with the *Foamville*, owned by Zillah Shipping Company, part of the Coast Lines group. The collision happened at Stockton Heath, Warrington. The *Mary P Cooper* suffered a large gash in her port side and sank on the southern side of the channel. The crew were all saved without injury, while the *Foamville* stood off upstream. The canal was blocked to all vessels apart from small coasters.

The *Mary P Cooper* had already had an extensive and exciting career. She was commissioned in 1896 as the *Owenabuee* for the Cork Harbour Commissioners as a grab hopper of 953 tons gross, although she was later used as a sand dredger. During the Irish Civil War the *Owenabuee* was commandeered, along with her sister ship the *Owenacurra*, by the Irish Republican Irregulars on 6 August 1922 and sunk as a blockship at the entrance to Cork Harbour. She was later raised and put back into service. Eventually she was sold to W. Cooper & Sons, Liverpool, in whose ownership she was at the time of the ship canal incident.

Before attempting to raise the *Mary P Cooper,* some of the sand was removed by *MSC Grab Hopper No 1*. This was followed by work to make the hold watertight. It was covered with wood planking and thick plywood and braced with twenty-one steel beams bolted across the deck. Large cylindrical flotation tanks were filled with water and attached to each side of the hull, and compressed air was then pumped into the tanks to expel the water and lift the wreck. Six weeks after the sinking, on 5 May 1961, the remains of the *Mary P Cooper* were towed into the old River Mersey channel behind Greenall's Avenue and beached. All fittings of any value were removed and she was abandoned as she lay.

Later the same year the Guinness boat *The Lady Gwendolen* was in collision with the Zillah Shipping Company's *Freshfield*. In this case, the owner of *The Lady Gwendolen* was found to be at fault as well as the master. It was ruled that an owner must be seen to own, manage and husband his ships correctly and safely and know what is going on.

The *Mary P Cooper* (1896), loaded with sand, sank at Stockton Heath, Warrington, on 21 March 1961 following collision with the coaster *Foamville*. The wreck blocked the canal to larger vessels for six weeks.

The Lady Grania (1952) and her sister *The Lady Gwendolen* (1953) were the first in the Guinness fleet to carry stout in 504-gallon cylindrical transportable tanks, seen here heading up the canal towards Barton Power Station. (Author)

In time this would be written into new legislation with further legal enforcements and consequences for all concerned, from the boardroom to the offending crew.

The *Freshfield*, 517 tons gross, was in course of a voyage from Par for Runcorn laden with 760 tons of china clay. Shortly before 7 a.m. on 10 November 1961, having crept up the channel from the Bar Light Vessel in reduced visibility, she reached a position where she was brought to anchor. At the time the *Freshfield* anchored she was in dense fog, and she immediately commenced to sound her bell. Shortly after the *Freshfield* had anchored, the hopper *Wirral* felt her way past and above her and let go her anchor a length or two above the position of the *Freshfield*. The *Wirral* also commenced and continued to sound her bell at the regulation intervals.

The Lady Gwendolen was in course of a voyage from Dublin for Liverpool laden with 642 tons of stout. On alternate voyages she would be destined for Manchester. The master, Captain Cecil Henry Meredith, came on to the bridge at about 5 a.m. when the vessel was passing the North West Float. The visibility at that time was about 2 miles and *The Lady Gwendolen* proceeded into and up the buoyed channels at her full speed of 10 knots. As she proceeded, the visibility reduced to about ¾ mile while the radar apparatus was set on the 3 mile range.

The Lady Gwendolen soon ran into dense fog and the master rang the engines to Stand By to alert the engineer to be ready at the controls. In the wheelhouse were the master and the helmsman; the spare man of the watch, who could be used as a lookout if necessary, was apparently aft in the mess room. Shortly after he rang Stand By, the master changed the setting of his radar from the 3 mile range to the 1 mile range and something over a minute later when, as he said, 'the picture established itself', he saw the echoes of the buoys on his starboard hand and 'two large but faint echoes just inside the buoyed channel'. Captain Meredith almost immediately afterwards saw 'the faint silhouette of the after part of what I now know to be the *Freshfield* close under my port bow'.

The soft nose of *The Lady Gwendolen* struck and rode over the starboard side of the *Freshfield* near her bridge, causing her to list violently to port. *The Lady Gwendolen* cleared by coming straight astern as the *Freshfield* started to sink rapidly. The master of the *Freshfield* immediately ordered his crew to abandon the vessel, and this they did by way of an inflatable life raft. All nine crew members were safely taken on board the *Wirral*, the master of which vessel used his twin screws to manoeuvre her while still anchored, so as to place his ship in a position to pick up the raft.

At the subsequent enquiry, the blame for the collision was found to fall 'wholly and heavily upon the master of *The Lady Gwendolen*'. He was proceeding at an excessive speed in fog in narrow and much-frequented waters with no lookout posted forward and no one on the bridge to keep a visual lookout while he, himself, was looking at the radar. Captain Meredith admitted at the enquiry 'that if I had not had radar, I would not have travelled at that speed'. The attitude of mind was 'that I can travel as fast as I like in fog and rely on a casual glance at my radar from time to time to keep me out of trouble'. It was found that Captain Meredith regularly exceeded speeds that would make for safe navigation. It was ruled that Author Guinness, Son & Company failed to ensure that the vessel's master took proper heed of safety at sea. In effect, the collision was the company's fault.

Manchester Liners suffered three fires during 1967 and 1968. The first was when the *Manchester Exporter*, the former *Cairndhu*, was 450 miles off the Irish coast with twelve passengers aboard. Drums of hydrogen peroxide had spilled onto combustible material, causing the fire in the hold to start. The crew were able to dowse the flames but sadly one of them died in the incident. The ship safely made her way to Belfast. A similar incident occurred to the *Manchester Merchant* when bales of nylon caught fire, but she too safely made it to port; in this case she docked at Halifax. The worst fire was on the *Manchester Miller* alongside at New York, attended by forty-two fire tenders and 200 firefighters. The water pumped into the ship caused a slight list as she settled to the bottom of the dock. Later raised, she was brought home and repaired. Thereafter she no longer carried passengers and some of the crew enjoyed the former passenger accommodation.

In March 1969 another serious accident happened, this time at Latchford Locks, as recorded in *Manchester Liners – An Extraordinary Story*:

The maiden voyage of the *Manchester Courage* was successfully completed and she sailed from Salford on her second trip on 16 March. Engine problems delayed her departure from No. 9 Dock and held up the departure of the *Governor* that was to follow down the Canal. That evening the '*Courage* had managed to get down to Irlam Lock with the Harrison liner hard on her heels, when the hydraulic system controlling the pitch on the propeller failed and the variable pitch propeller automatically assumed its default position in forward thrust mode. With the stern tug already let go for passage into the adjacent small lock the new ship inevitably hit the downstream

The *Manchester Exporter* (1952) coming up the canal below the Warburton High Level Bridge. She was previously Cairn Lines' *Cairndhu*. (Author)

gate. The force of the impact was such that the integrity of the gate was breached. It was not feasible to close the upstream gate with the flow of water passing down the lock and the level of the canal was lowered all the way back to Barton Lock. Fortunately the *Governor* was still safely above Barton.

The *Manchester Courage* ended up half in and half out of the lock. When she was removed and inspected, it was found that the hull was undamaged but she remained trapped in the canal until the new gates could be installed and the canal level reinstated. Although lightly loaded, she did have 3,650 mailbags on board. These and other cargo were removed by crane and sent to Liverpool to be loaded on the hastily chartered container ship *Hother Isle*. Thereafter, standing instructions for the *Manchester Courage* class of ship were to disengage the engine while in the ship canal locks.

Then there was the Bob's Ferry tragedy, which occurred early in the morning of 24 April 1970. The Dutch tanker *Tacoma* had been loading petrol at Partington. Safety instructions were that two watchmen be present to ensure that overflowing tanks were avoided. However, the two men went to the canteen for tea and were away from their posts for over four hours. Meanwhile 14,000 gallons of petrol was discharged directly into the canal. Being lighter than water, it floated on the canal surface and flowed both up and down the canal. The young ferryman at Bob's Ferry had taken his first load of workers across the canal at 5.30 a.m. and had then suspended the ferry to await advice as he was worried about the strong smell and the vapour rising off the canal. Meanwhile workers on the other bank, worried they would be late for work, commandeered the spare ferry boat and started to row across the canal. The ferryman realised they were putting into danger and set off to warn them. Before he was able to get to the men there was a huge explosion, in which five of the men died immediately and one other later in hospital.

Despite all these major incidents and the Bob's Ferry tragedy, business carried on in the canal. Tonnage handled declined from 18 million in 1960 to 16 million in 1970, a drop that would continue thereafter at an increasing rate due to a variety of factors, but principally dictated by economies of scale whereby most ocean-going ships became too large to navigate the canal, coupled with dock labour problems.

The widest ship ever to come up to Manchester was Strick Line's *Serbistan*, which made the trip as a brand new ship in 1966. She was completed in March 1966 with a beam of 63 feet 10 inches, allowing just 7 inches of water either side in the locks above Eastham. Her trip was obviously trouble-free as she returned to Manchester on two more occasions.

Labour relations were an increasing problem both at sea and ashore in the 1960s. An unofficial strike by seamen in summer 1960 lasted six weeks before the men went back to work. This meant that British ships arriving at Manchester were strikebound until the dispute ended. The National Union of Seamen's strike in 1966, which lasted from 16 May to 1 July, saw many more ships idle in the docks at Manchester and along the canal-side wharfs. Ships were moored two deep adjacent to Pier 6 between Nos 6 and 7 docks, and included four members of the Manchester Liners fleet, one Clan Line vessel, one of the Prince Line's motor ships, and Transatlantic Carriers' *Caxton*.

On the other side of No. 7 Dock was one of the Furness Pacific ships and British & Continental's motor ship *Egret*. All were moored with bows pointing to the end of the dock, as was always the custom at Manchester. At the same time, dockers were on strike in Canada, causing a particularly hard time for Manchester Liners.

Another problem, albeit one that would take a while to impact traffic statistics at Manchester, was the closure of the Suez Canal in 1967 during the conflict between Israel and Egypt. The Suez Canal did not reopen for a further seven years, during which time larger ships were of necessity deployed on the longer alternative routes via the Cape or Panama. This meant that an increasing number of ships deployed on the Gulf, Far East and Australasian services were too large to access Manchester.

With Manchester Liners running its big steamers up the St Lawrence Seaway to Great Lakes ports each summer, it suffered a shortage of tonnage. The small Lakers had done their job and were disposed of, and even the intermediate sized motor ships *Manchester Faith* and *Manchester Fame* had become too small for the trade. The fleet was developed by the introduction of the big engines-aft motor ships of the *Manchester Commerce* Class and subsequently by the improved *Manchester Port* and *Manchester Progress*, and capable of carrying standard 20-foot-long containers.

Perhaps the most exciting development of the decade was the arrival of the fully cellular container ship and the special facilities built to handle the containers. Manchester Liners decided to go it alone with fully cellular ships and focus on its core Manchester to Montreal route. The *Manchester Courage*, which hit the lock gate at Latchford, was the second of a group of six sisters built at Smiths Dock Middlesbrough for the company. The first ship in the class was the *Manchester Challenge*. The ships were ice-strengthened to allow an all-year-round service. The contract for the first three ships and 4,500 containers was placed at a cost of £100 million. They were scheduled to arrive in Montreal 6½ days after leaving Eastham and by 1970 there was a scheduled departure every 4½ days. When the full complement of container ships was in place, this increased to two departures a week from both Montreal and Manchester.

The *Manchester Challenge* took her maiden voyage in November 1968 under the command of Captain Phillip Fielding. She ploughed through the winter ice into Montreal, unloaded and reloaded in two days before returning to the ice fields of the St Lawrence. The *Manchester Courage* was delivered in February 1969 and the *Manchester Concorde* in May. In 1970, the ugly duckling *Manchester Miller* was made uglier still when she was converted to a fully cellular ship and renamed *Manchester Quest*. The ships were serviced at Manchester at a new container terminal at the end of No. 9 Dock, to which a second gantry crane was added in 1971 along with an extension of the quay to accommodate two ships at the same time. In the meantime, the conventional 'container-friendly' ships operated by Manchester Liners continued to serve the ports in the Great Lakes.

The Furness Pacific service via Panama to Vancouver closed in November 1970. The service had suffered from dock strikes both at home and abroad, coupled with rising costs of port labour in the United States. Increasing competition from foreign flag operators and the onset of containerisation spelled the end. The post-war-built

'BUSINESS AS USUAL'

Above: A rare visitor was J. Bruce & Company's *Alhama* (1948), working on a joint service to the Mediterranean with Ellerman. She is seen inbound below Irwell Park Wharf.

Below: The *Ebro* (1952) discharging bulk sulphur at Irwell Park Wharf. (Author)

Opposite above: The *Burutu Palm* (1952) was an infrequent visitor to the canal and was one of the Palm Line ships based at Bromborough operating to West Africa. She is seen here coming down the canal above Barton in July 1962. (Author)

Opposite middle: T. & J. Brocklebank's *Makrana* (1957), minus most of her funnel, coming up the canal above Barton Locks in May 1962. (Author)

Opposite below: The *Temple Main* (1958) was one of Lambert Brothers' small tramp ships and is seen going down the canal above Runcorn in May 1967. (Author)

The *Manchester Fame* (1959), passing down the canal below Barton Road Bridge. She and sister ship *Manchester Faith* (1959) were the last of Manchester's small Great Lakes ships when Manchester Liners sold them in 1970. (Author)

The *Manchester Challenge* (1968) leaving Latchford Lock on her way down the canal in August 1973. (Author)

Pacific Unity and *Pacific Fortune* were sold in 1964 and 1965 respectively, and were not replaced as the service was then maintained collaboratively with other owners operating to other UK ports. The remaining four ships, the *Pacific Reliance*, *Pacific Northwest*, *Pacific Envoy* and *Pacific Stronghold*, were transferred into the Royal Mail Line fleet on the closure of the service without change of name. Three of them were sold the following year to Greek shipowners, although all of them had been resold for demolition by 1974, while the oldest of the quartet, the *Pacific Reliance*, was sold directly for breaking up in 1970.

Clan Line still regularly used Manchester throughout the 1960s for its services to South Africa and the Far East. A new and highly mechanised transit shed was built for the company at the head of No. 6 Dock. The shed was opened in 1967 when the *Clan Graham* berthed alongside on 6 July.

Harrison Line still also loaded for Manchester from a variety of east coast African ports, the Gulf and South Asia. This combination of loading led to interesting calculations being made to balance unloading and reloading at UK ports to ensure that the vessels' draught and air draught would permit passage along the Manchester Ship Canal. Harrisons continued to upgrade its fleet with new ships.

The Prince Line Mediterranean service had run into trouble by the mid-1960s, when it started to make a loss. This was partly due to the design of the ships, with extensive gross tonnage devoted to just twelve passengers. In 1968 the goodwill of the Manchester to Mediterranean service of Prince Line was bought by Manchester Liners to form the Manchester Prince Line. The Prince Line loading brokers at Manchester was also taken over and the ships sold. In their stead, three small motor cargo ships were taken on charter: Coast Lines' *Lancashire Coast* and *Cheshire Coast* became the *Trojan Prince* and *Spartan Prince* while the British & Continental company's motor ship *Egret*, completed for them in 1959, became the *Tartar Prince*. Coast Lines' *Adriatic Coast* also did one round trip to the Mediterranean in February 1968, wearing full Coast Lines livery but flying the Prince Line flag.

The British & Continental Steamship Company had progressively downsized. It maintained its services largely with chartered tonnage. The services to the Low Countries became unviable as shippers preferred to use the roll-on roll-off ferry services, sending lorry-loads of goods to the Continent. British & Continental ceased to trade in June 1968 when it became a subsidiary of its Dutch partner, van Ommeren. When the *Tartar Prince* (*Egret*) was off-chartered in 1972 she was sold.

Another company that ceased trading in the 1960s was Transatlantic Carriers. The company's ships had been managed by Walter Runciman & Company, but in 1962 Runciman was dismissed and replaced by in-house management under the trading banner Canatlantic. The funnel colours were changed to an attractive solid green and black top separated by a broad white band. But two years later the steamers *Caslon* and *Isaac Carter* were sold and replaced by just one motor ship, the *Aragona*. She had been built in 1956 for Finnish owners and had an ice-strengthened hull. The steamer *Baskerville* was sold in 1967 and not replaced, while the motor ships *Caxton* and the newly acquired *Aragona* were sold the following year, and the company ceased trading.

The *Trojan Prince* (1954) was chartered for the Manchester Prince Line service to the Mediterranean in 1968; she was otherwise Coast Lines' *Lancashire Coast* and is seen outbound just above Barton Lock on 7 April 1968. (Author)

Bowater commissioned its last ship in 1961. This was the *Nina Bowater*, the sixth and last of the 4,000 ton gross *Elizabeth Bowater* Class of pulp and paper carriers. The older ships *Liverpool Packet*, *Markland* and *Liverpool Rover* were sold out of the fleet by 1963. Five years later it was the turn of the turbine steamers: these were increasingly uneconomical and the *Margaret Bowater* was sold in 1968, followed by the *Sarah Bowater*; they were both broken up by 1971. The first of the motor ships to be sold out of the fleet was the *Alice Bowater*, which went to Canadian buyers in 1969. In their stead, Bowater increasingly chartered in specialist ships to carry raw products to the British mills, including the newsprint mill at Ellesmere Port, and to carry finished products to their buyers.

The Bowater ships were always a welcome sight in the canal and alongside the Bowater Wharf at Ellesmere Port, owing to their distinctive livery. This comprised a Brunswick green hull, originally with pale-green boot topping but replaced by red in the early 1960s as the colour was difficult to maintain, and cream upperworks. The funnel was a dull yellow with the distinctive trademark bow and arrow over wavy blue water device of the Bowater Corporation. The trademark was also proudly displayed on the bow of each ship. The ships were always immaculately turned out. Discharging and loading completed at Ellesmere Port, they were turned off the Stanlow Oil Dock and returned down the canal to Eastham.

One issue at the Bowater Wharf was the narrowness of the channel and the speed of passing ships. A regular insurance claim was that of ships moored at the berth being pulled off the quay by the suction caused by passing ships. Standing orders in

Typical of the *Elizabeth Bowater* Class of newsprint and pulp carrier was the *Constance Bowater* (1958).

Harrison Line ships included a watch by the third officer, stationed on the stern, on the behaviour of ships alongside the Bowater Wharf to record if they looked as though they had swung off the quay after the Harrison ship had passed. Canal pilots were well aware of the issue, however, and big ships generally passed the Bowater Wharf at 'dead slow'.

In the mid-1960s an agreement was made between James Fisher & Son of Barrow, a long-established short-sea cargo operator, and the Central Electricity Generating Board to build two heavy-lift ships for domestic trade. The ships were commissioned in 1966 and were named the *Aberthaw Fisher* and *Kingsnorth Fisher*, reflecting the charterer's interest in power stations under construction on the coast. Their role was to carry up to three 300-ton units of heavy machinery, built largely at Manchester, to the various coastal power station construction sites.

The *Aberthaw Fisher* and *Kingsnorth Fisher* had a hold accessed by a lift for smaller units, including low-loader vehicles. A special roll-on berth was built for them at Pomona Docks, where the twins were based, and a similar structure was made at Barry Docks when the ships brought equipment for the nearby Aberthaw power station. The ships were broad in the beam for their size in order to offer stability for heavy loads stowed on the strengthened main deck. They had twin screws to aid manoeuvrability in confined shallow waters, and were also of surprisingly shallow draught to enable them to access temporary shore facilities adjacent to construction sites. They were, however, quite wet ships and tended to run for shelter in anything approaching Force 5 or 6 winds.

The heavy lift ship *Aberthaw Fisher* (1966) was owned by James Fisher & Sons and chartered to the Central Electricity Generating Board. Her role was to ship heavy machinery built at Manchester to the various coastal power stations under construction in the late 1960s.

The Lady Patricia (1963) was a bulk stout carrier owned by Arthur Guinness. She is seen above the Barton Swing Aqueduct, heading up to the Guinness wharf, which was then just below Mode Wheel. (Author)

The Guinness boats still came up to Manchester, but to a new terminal below Mode Wheel where they discharged the casks of stout onto road trailers. The new *The Lady Patricia* was commissioned in December 1962 and the old steamer *Guinness*, which had served the company so well since 1931, was sold for demolition a few months later once the new ship had settled in to trade. *The Lady Grania* and *The Lady Gwendolen* continued in service.

Another cable-laying ship came up to Manchester in 1964 to load cable manufactured by British Insulated Callenders Cables at Trafford Park. The *Photinia* was chartered from Stag Line and adapted to carry out the cable-laying over her bows. The cable was laid between Oteranga Bay, North Island, New Zealand, and Fighting Bay, South Island. Another power cable was laid by *Photinia* between the islands of Trinidad and Tobago in 1965.

In 1966, Philmac (Phillips Petroleum & Macadam) opened a new specialist refinery at Eastham that brought the *London Splendour* to the Queen Elizabeth II terminal on 27 April 1966 with the first consignment of crude oil for the plant. Smaller parcel tankers tended to frequent the canal but the larger tankers were becoming a thing of the past.

The 1960s was a period when Manchester could have done much more to safeguard its customer base. The Manchester Ship Canal did not control its dock workers, who worked under the auspices of the National Dock Labour Board. The National Dock Strike in 1967 was disruptive enough, but a major outcome of it was that all dockers now had jobs for life. The conundrum was that cargo handling was becoming less

The parcel tanker *Irish Holly* (1954) in the shadow of the old Barton power station, coming up the canal to the Mode Wheel terminal in July 1966. (Author)

F. T. Everard's tanker *Allurity* (1969) coming up through the Barton Bridges on a dull day in December 1970. (Author)

labour intensive with increased use of pallets and containers. Bulk handling had already become mechanised and streamlined. As jobs became fewer, discontent inevitably rose among the workforce, leading to a series of lightning strikes in the early 1970s that conspired to drive clients away from the Port of Manchester. On top of all this, the container ship was set to grow in size, diverting traffic from Manchester to the ports of Felixstowe, London, Southampton and Liverpool where the larger ships could dock. The traditional business of the Port of Manchester was set to decline rapidly in the 1970s, a decline that was exacerbated by the intransigence of the dockers and their frequent withdrawals of labour.

Chapter 12

No More Ships at Manchester

On 28 July 1972, the nation's dock workers went on strike in an attempt to safeguard their jobs. They were protesting at plans for compulsory redundancies and threats to their workload from container firms using cheaper, casual labour, particularly at the new inland container depots. The strike was exactly what Manchester could not afford; it had weathered the earlier strikes, but the absence of dock labour for nearly four weeks was crippling. The writing was on the wall, certainly for the main Manchester dock system as more and more companies turned their backs on Manchester. The ship canal company had done everything it could to help keep the port abreast of new needs. The container terminal at No. 9 Dock was followed by a new container terminal at Ellesmere Port, while major investment went into dredging to maintain the depth of water needed for the larger ships to actually get up to Manchester.

Quite a number of shipowners transferred their allegiance to Ellesmere Port in the early 1970s. A company new to the ship canal was the Ellerman City Mediterranean service, which initially moved from Liverpool to Garston, where it shared a container facility with Cawood Containers. Ellerman then employed the small container ships of the so-called *Hustler* Class, but the new Garston container facility suffered from dock labour issues. In May 1972, Cawood moved to a new specially built container handling wharf and depot at Ellesmere Port, taking with it Ellerman's newly formed joint service with Moss Hutchison and Zim Line to Israel. Ellerman's Portugal trade also moved to Ellesmere Port in July, followed by the Italian trade shortly afterwards, so bringing a totally new regime into the Port of Manchester. The quay was extended in 1986 to 790 feet while the terminal area was also expanded.

Guinness boats moved from Mode Wheel to Runcorn in the early 1970s. In 1974 *The Lady Patricia* was converted into a tanker with fixed stainless steel tanks to carry the stout, rather than the traditional uplifting and discharging of large casks. The stout was discharged into road tankers. *The Lady Grania* was sold in 1974, while *The Lady Gwendolen* survived in the Guinness fleet until 1977, when she too was sold and replaced by the *Miranda Guinness*, another bulk stout tanker. The *Miranda Guinness* stayed in trade until 1993, when she was sold, only to be broken up at Liverpool the following year. Also in 1993, *The Lady Patricia* was sold to be broken up at Manchester when Guinness ceased to be shipowners and instead brought its stout to England in road tankers aboard conventional Irish Sea vehicle ferries.

Manchester Liners' profits dwindled so that by 1971 the company was in need of reforming to get back into profit. Like the *Manchester Miller* before her, the *Manchester Progress* was converted into a fully cellular container ship and renamed *Manchester Concept* in 1971. By 1973 the last of the conventional ships had been sold; their role in serving the Great Lakes ports was taken over from 1970 by the small container ship *Manchester Merit*, which was purchased on the stocks to run a feeder service to Montreal. In the winter she crossed the Atlantic to work on the Manchester Prince Line service to the Mediterranean. In 1972, two chartered container ships took over the Montreal feeder service and the *Manchester Merit* was demise chartered-out, but still served in the Great Lakes during the summer season. Her role on the new Mediterranean container service was now taken by the *Frontier*, which was joined the following year by the *Manchester Zeal* and *Manchester Vigour*, the three ships offering a fully containerised service to the Mediterranean under the Manchester Prince Line banner. The ships wore the Manchester Liners livery of orange-red hull and white upperworks.

In June 1973, Manchester Liners started a weekly service from Rotterdam and Felixstowe to Montreal in a bid to woo back its Continental clients. The service was not a success but CP Ships (formerly Canadian Pacific) was persuaded to leave Liverpool and concentrate on London if Manchester Liners left Felixstowe. This it did, with improved business prospects for Manchester. Two further *Manchester Challenge* Class ships were commissioned for the charter market in 1974, the *Manchester Reward* and *Manchester Renown*. When they finally came off charter in the depressed trading conditions of the late 1970s, the older *Manchester Challenge* and *Manchester Courage* were sold. Furness Withy had again become a majority shareholder in Manchester Liners, which was now its sole operator on the North Atlantic.

Manchester Liners continued to be dogged by industrial problems. For example, it carried the following advertisement in the *Montreal Gazette* on 22 April 1975 (note that turn-around times at Toronto and Halifax were not even guessed at):

Due to strike conditions prevailing at St Lawrence River ports the schedule of sailings listed below should be used as a guide only. Vessels have been rerouted to alternative ports and at the time of going to press longshore labour have stated they will not work the vessels:

From Manchester 20 March *Manchester Challenge* eta. Toronto 11 April
From Manchester 28 March *Manchester Concorde* eta. Halifax 11 April
From Manchester 15 April *Manchester Crusade* eta. Montreal 22 April ets. 24 April
From Manchester 18 April *Manchester Courage* eta. Montreal 25 April ets. 27 April

In February 1980, Furness Withy sold out to C. Y. Tung of Hong Kong with promises that Manchester Liners would remain intact. Within a year the *Manchester Vigour*

The small container ship *Manchester Zeal* (1973) coming into Eastham Lock from the Mersey.

The *Manchester Reward* (1974) approaching Eastham Lock.

and *Manchester Zeal* were sold, leaving the Mediterranean service in the hands of chartered ships. In August 1981, Manchester Liners became part of a consortium working out of Felixstowe to Montreal and its bigger ships no longer came to Manchester. Indeed, they were too large for the canal. In 1983 the Manchester Prince Line, which had already transferred to Ellesmere Port, joined up with Ellerman's City Line and Zim Israel Navigation Line to form a new co-ordinated container service to the Mediterranean. By 1988 the Mediterranean service had disappeared into the Tung empire, the Montreal interests were absorbed into Orient Overseas Container Line and Manchester Liners was no more.

The Manchester container wharf was no longer in business; the docks effectively closed to trading in 1982. Plans were put in hand to develop the dock estate for a variety of industrial, residential and leisure purposes in collaboration with Salford Corporation.

But what of all the other shipping companies that used to frequent Manchester? The Clan Line used its new facilities at No. 6 Dock only infrequently and took its last sailing from Manchester in 1977. The Anchor Line still came up to Manchester but on an irregular basis as cargo inducement allowed. The last Anchor Line ship to come up to Manchester was the *Egidia* in 1977, and she was only on bareboat charter to Anchor.

T. & J. Brocklebank, along with its owners Cunard, was taken over by investment and property development company Trafalgar House in 1971. Rationalisation followed, with ten ships sold within the year and a further one ship chartered out. This left just six ships to maintain the Indian service, which had been merged with those of P&O and British India following the takeover. Thereafter, none of the remaining Brocklebank ships came up to Manchester. By mid-1983 the fleet had gone.

The Strick Line continued to berth its Persian Gulf service at Manchester until 1972, when the company was finally taken over by P&O. It had long been a member of the P&O Group but until now not a wholly owned subsidiary. The elderly triple steam expansion and low-pressure turbine steamer *Tangistan*, a familiar sight on the canal, was sold and the remaining members of the fleet disappeared into the P&O General Cargo Division, never again to call at Manchester.

The Harrison Line pooled its resources with Ellerman City Liners to build a 53,790 gross ton container ship, the *City of Durban*, for the South Africa service. She was delivered in February 1978. This new service was created at the expense of the conventional ships, so that by the end of 1978 Harrison had totally withdrawn from Manchester.

The end of the Bowater Steamship Company was recorded by Chief Officer David Hawker in *Sea Breezes* in November 1977:

At 13.30 on 20 May last the ensign of the motor ship *Nina Bowater* was lowered and she became the *Kretan Glory* under the Greek flag. It was a sad moment for me, as chief officer, because she was the last ship of the Bowater Steamship Company. With the advent of ro-ro ships, a new fleet of pulp and paper carrier has been built, but sadly this has not been a British company.

Anchor Line's *Egidia* (1961) lying in No. 9 Dock ahead of one of the Clan Line ships of the *Clan Macnab* Class in 1977. The tour boat *MSC Silver Arrow II* (1969) is in the foreground.

Harrison Line's *Explorer* (1961) approaching Barton Swing Aqueduct on her way down the canal on 10 April 1970. (Author)

Bulk grain imports still came up the canal in the early 1970s, generally in tramp steamers chartered for single voyages. Indeed, one of the former Prince Line ships, built under licence during the Second World War as the *English Prince*, brought a bulk grain cargo to Manchester in August 1970 when she was the Greek-owned *Simos*. As the *English Prince,* she generally served between New York and South Africa and was not one of the Manchester-based ships. The bulk grain imports diminished during the decade in favour of split cargoes bought up from the Seaforth Grain Terminal at Liverpool. However, Cerestar (Grain Products) chartered the British-registered 3,645 gross ton bulk carrier *Ringnes* for several trips bringing grain from Europe to the former Brown & Polson Wharf at Manchester in the mid-1970s.

H. Watson & Company (see Chapters 5 and 9) made one last attempt at operating a shipping service in 1981. It formed a joint venture with MAT to charter vessels for a UK to the United States Gulf service under the banner Watson-MAT Line. It operated from Ellesmere Port, running to Houston, New Orleans and Mobile. Trading conditions at that time were difficult; the service was not a success and was closed in 1982.

In March 1981, the ship canal company handed the remnants of its tug fleet, four V-Class motor tugs, to Carmet Tugs to manage and operate. At the same time the dredging responsibility was given to Westminster Dredging, allowing a lot of small tugs, lighters and dredgers to be sold. The pilotage service had always operated with self-employed staff, so little by little the ship canal company distanced itself from the day to day operation of the canal.

In December 1972 a new molten sulphur unloading and storage facility had been opened at Runcorn. Imports were brought in by small chemical tankers, but by the mid-1980s four Polish-owned sulphur tankers of nearly 10,000 tons deadweight were in use importing up to 200,000 tons per year of molten sulphur from Gdansk. The ships' names did not roll off the tongue quite so easily as many of their forebears: *Tarnobrzeg, Professor K Bohdanowicz, Zaglebie Starkowe* and *Siarkopol*. Small petrochemical tankers continued to come up the canal until the mid-1970s, when that trade ceased.

Philmac continued to import crude oil to its Eastham refinery using its dedicated tanker, the *Philmac Venture*. The *Philmac Venture* had a gross tonnage of 20,952, was built in Japan and arrived at Eastham on her maiden voyage on 14 February 1983. She was sold in 1987, having made over forty voyages into Eastham.

After the last parts of the Manchester docks system closed in 1982, the whole area was redeveloped, initially including an enterprise zone. Ship canal company chairman Donald Redford wrote in the *Port of Manchester Review 1981*:

In such circumstances it is only human nature to think back to the past, the so-called good old days. The trouble is we tend to remember the good times, rarely the bad. Many people will recall the years when everything seemed settled and solid, and ships lay double-banked at Manchester berths, and others queued up outside waiting to get in. Today, due to changing patterns of trade and the economic recession, the picture is very different. But things are stirring in the newly designated enterprise zone, and the lower reaches of the Canal are busy.

The coaster *Seaforth Trader* (1952), seen at Latchford on 3 April 1974, was owned by Bulk Cargo Handling Services of Liverpool and brought grain up to Manchester. (Author)

Just a memory: the coastal tanker *Alacrity* (1966), owned by F. T. Everard & Sons, coming up the canal having just left Latchford Lock in April 1974. (Author)

The *Esso Purfleet* (1967), carrying one of the last oil imports to the upper part of the canal, seen below the Barton High Level Bridge. (Author)

Ships came to Manchester no more. Although, as Chairman Redford reported, the docks at Runcorn and Ellesmere Port remained vibrant with various trades set to continue. In 1991 the Manchester Ship Canal Company sold out to Peel Holdings, finally amalgamating the interests of Manchester and Liverpool, an amalgamation that had been threatened before but one which had been anathema to Manchester for the previous 100 years. Now, however, it made sense; Manchester would retain its petrochemical trade to Stanlow and its general cargo trade to Ellesmere Port. Little traffic was expected to penetrate the canal beyond Runcorn.

In October 2007 a new container shuttle service was commenced by Peel Ports between the Seaforth Container Terminal at Liverpool and the new Irlam Container Terminal, later rebranded Port Salford. The shuttle started as a three times a week service utilising a pusher tug, the *Daisy Doardo*, and a barge capable of carrying 160 containers. The service was upgraded to a small 3,125 tons gross container ship, the *Coastal Deniz*, which carried up to 260 containers, calling at intermediate berths along the canal as required. Increased capacity is now provided by the *Thea II*, which can carry 340 containers. Some 30,000 containers came into the canal in 2014, a tenfold increase on the volume of traffic in 2009.

A visit to some of the publicly accessible inland locks and bridges across the canal in March 2015 revealed an image almost of dereliction. All the bridges were badly in need of repainting, while Latchford Locks has clearly become a focus for graffiti. The derelict high level railway bridge at Latchford looked as if a high wind might even bring bits of it down! B&Q now occupy the site of the former power station at Barton, while the refinery and tank farm across the Bridgwater Canal at Barton has

The brand new Norwegian chemical tanker *Brage Baltic* (1980) arriving at the Ince Oil Berth on 3 January 1981 at the start of an extensive charter to Shell. She was owned by K/S Bras A/S Vi of Bergen and managed by Rederiet S. Bartz Johannessen A/S. (Shell UK Oil)

Barton, March 2015, a derelict scene of the bridges badly in need of a coat of paint, the aqueduct drained, no ships, nobody… (Author)

been flattened preparatory to redevelopment. What will become of the canal in the future remains to be seen, but one small container ship every few days does not pay for the upkeep of the canal above Runcorn.

The prize for Manchester's most innovative ship must be awarded to Manchester Liners' cellular container ship the *Manchester Challenge*, the first of six almost identical sisters designed to carry 535 20-foot containers. The *Manchester Challenge* was launched into the Tees at Middlesbrough in June 1968 and departed Manchester on her maiden voyage to Montreal in November. Andrew Bell described the ship in an article in *Ships Monthly* in February 2011:

A total deadweight of 12,000 tons could be carried on a draught of 27 feet. There was bridge control on the main engines and the engine room could be unmanned; all maintenance was done during the Manchester turn round when the ship was coupled to shore power supplies ... Two twenty foot containers of stores were loaded and stored through their own hatch located just ahead of the accommodation block; for the voyage they became the ship's stores. Under the upper deck and running the length of the ship on the outboard side was a working alleyway to starboard and a pipe and cable one to port. There was no need to brave the weather by going on deck to reach the forecastle where the mooring arrangements were located under the forecastle head. If there was a snowstorm in Montreal's winter the mooring equipment and the windlass did not need to be excavated before they could be used.

The *Manchester Challenge* Class carried a crew of just twenty-seven, and they were accommodated in spacious accommodation. However, the ships soon became outdated as scale demanded larger and larger container ships, funded not by one company but by a large consortia of companies. Victims of their own success, the new container ships were to desert the new terminal at Manchester in the late 1970s.

Pomona Docks even had its own floating restaurant and pub in the 1970s. The *North Westward Ho!* was bought by Jud Evans in October 1972, and after permission was granted the ship was brought up the ship canal and berthed at Pomona. Seven plush bars, a restaurant and a venue room were built into what had originally been the Isle of Wight Ferry *Vecta*, built in 1938, and latterly the excursion ship *Westward Ho!*. A late-night licence and disco led to the success of the venture. A veteran Comet jet was purchased from the RAF and parked next door as an overflow venue, complete with dance floor. The ship became too expensive to maintain in the early 1980s and the business was closed; she was then towed to Bromborough Dock on 19 March 1985, later moved to London and again to Cornwall, where she was declared beyond repair and demolished in 1997.

The day cruise along the Manchester Ship Canal has always been popular both from an educational viewpoint and as a leisure activity. In the 1950s, the cruise was resurrected on selected weekends by the Co-operative Travel Service using the Seacombe ferry *Egremont*. A typical schedule for the trip down the canal was embarkation at Pomona Docks from the Cornbrook Road Entrance from 9.30 a.m. and on completion of boarding:

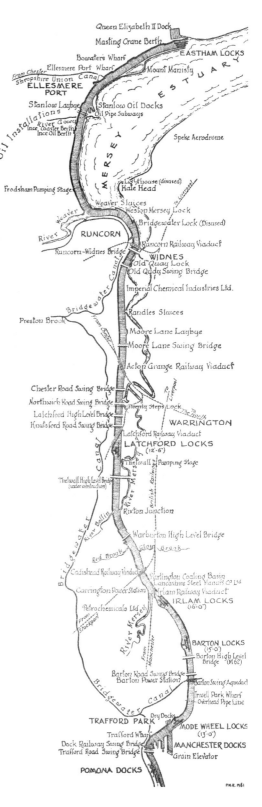

Map of the Manchester Ship Canal
from a 1961 Co-operative Travel Service
souvenir ticket for the cruise from
Manchester Pomona Docks to New
Brighton.

Co-operative Travel Service organised Manchester and New Brighton cruises via the Manchester Ship Canal during the late 1950s and early 1960s with the Mersey ferry *Egremont* (1951).

TSMV *Egremont* leaves for New Brighton via the Manchester Ship Canal and Mersey Estuary. 4.00 pm (approx.) passengers disembark at New Brighton. Passengers leave New Brighton by Ferry Steamer in time to connect with through trains from Liverpool Central to Manchester Central ...

The trip is even more popular today aboard the contemporary Mersey ferries, even though there is usually no other shipping to be seen on the canal above Runcorn and precious little below.

The Manchester Ship Canal Company was a fabulous wealth creator for the North West, but it took many decades before it was able to return a worthwhile dividend to its shareholders. Wooing new business by waiving canal dues, coupled with the continuous expense of dredging, weighed heavily on the purse in the early days. In later years the ongoing expense of dredging, combined with the need to upgrade facilities and equipment, was also a heavy burden. Only between 1969 and 1978 did the company manage to pay a respectable dividend to its 14,000 shareholders. Above all, the Manchester Ship Canal and its owning company were seen as symbols of Mancunian determination. The canal remains today as a magnificent artefact, saluting a grand style of Victorian engineering.

Bibliography

Bruce, Warren, *With the Manchester Ship Canal Company* (Radcliffe, Neil Richardson, 1990).

Burrell, David, *Furness Withy: The Centenary History of Furness Withy and Company 1891–1991* (Kendal, World Ship Society, 1992).

Burrell, David, 'Manchester Liners Ltd', in Roy Fenton & John Clarkson (eds), *British Shipping Fleets* (Longton, Ships in Focus Publications, 2000).

Farnie, Douglas, *The Manchester Ship Canal and the Rise of the Port of Manchester 1894–1975* (Manchester, Manchester University Press, 1980).

Hyde, Francis, *Blue Funnel: A History of Alfred Holt & Company of Liverpool from 1865 to 1914* (Liverpool, Liverpool University Press, 1956).

Leech, Bosdin, *History of the Manchester Ship Canal, From its Inception to its Completion, with Personal Reminiscences*, volumes 1 and 2 (Manchester and London, Sherratt & Hughes, 1907).

MANCHESTER EDUCATION COMMITTEE, *The Inland Port of Manchester, its Ships and their Cargoes* (Manchester, The Port of Manchester Committee of the Manchester Chamber of Commerce, 1938).

Robins, Nick, *Manchester Liners – An Extraordinary Story* (Portishead, Bernard McCall, 2011).

Robins, Nick, *The Tyne-Tees Steam Shipping Company and its Associates* (Portishead, Bernard McCall, 2014).

Sinclair, Robert, *Across the Irish Sea, Belfast–Liverpool Shipping since 1819* (London, Conway Maritime Press, 1990).

Stoker, Robert, *Sixty Years on the Western Ocean* (Manchester, Manchester Liners Ltd, 1959).

Taylor, James, *Ellermans, a Wealth of Shipping* (London, Wilton House Gentry, 1976).

Whatley Merita, *Point Arena lighthouse* (Mount Pleasant SC, Arcadia Publishing, 2013).

Also available from Amberley Publishing

Preston
Planes, Trains, Tramcars and Ships
David John Hindle

A fascinating look at Preston's transport heritage and the many ways in which the town
contributed to British transport history.

978-1-4456-4381-6
128 pages, illustrated throughout

Available from all good bookshops or to order direct
Please call **01453–847–800**
www.amberley-books.com

Also available from Amberley Publishing

The Great Brunel
Chris Morris

Chris Morris tracks down Brunel's legacy to provide an unrivalled visual celebration of the great man and his work.

978-1-4456-5079-1
128 pages, illustrated throughout

Available from all good bookshops or to order direct
Please call **01453-847-800**
www.amberleybooks.com

Also available from Amberley Publishing

On Tour with Thomas Telford
Chris Morris

A visual celebration of Telford's architectural and engineering legacy, from the mighty Menai Bridge to the harbours, manses and chapels of the remote Scottish Highlands.

978-1-4456-5057-9

160 pages, illustrated throughout

Available from all good bookshops or to order direct
Please call **01453-847-800**
www.amberleybooks.com